THE HAIR EMPIRE CEO

How to Start a Hair Extension Business with Little to No Money

DENISE FONWEBAN

~ *Copyright, Disclaimer & Legal* ~

~ *Dedication* ~

This book is dedicated to everyone reading this book right now and either looking to start a hair business empire from scratch, or looking for tips and strategies to help grow and move their existing hair business forward. I hope you enjoy reading this book and find value in it as much as I enjoyed writing it.

Denise.xx

~ *Contents* ~

Part 1

GETTING
STARTED

INTRODUCTION

Approximately $19 billion is spent annually on hair weave and extensions in the USA whilst in the UK, £7.25 billion is the annual spend - and UK black women account for 80% of total hair product sales. Weaves, wigs and hair extensions however seem to be here to stay - and the more real looking the hair, the better. Mintel reports "nearly 6 out of 10 black consumers wear a wig, weave or extensions, which enables them to switch up their look". For most black women, it's ALL about being able to change their looks and extensions are a more manageable way to do this.

Hair is an important aspect of Black female culture, so it's unsurprising that that much money is spent on hair. And it isn't just the black women, but white and Caucasian women who are now obsessed with fusion bonded hair, lace front wigs and clip in extensions.

This could be those clips -in extensions to give them a more glamorous look for night outs and special occasions, or fusion bonded hair for a more day to day glamorous look.

So what does this mean for you?

This means, you have the potential to start a business in an industry that is already very lucrative and therefore a potential to market yourself and make some really good money if you really put your mind to it.

Women are prepared to pay anything for their beauty and looks, that's a fact! Meaning as a hair extension business owner, there's always going to be a need for your product every single time.

Overall human hair extensions are a booming industry and will always be. Hence it is no wonder more and more people are taking advantage of this opportunity and tapping into this hair industry pie.

When I started my online hair brand Yes Weave in 2016, one of my biggest challenges was finding a manual or at least a guide that could teach me step by step how to start my own hair business from scratch. Google was swamped with different sources of irrelevant information, with no direct relevance to starting a hair extension business.

Of course this made the whole process of starting my business confusing and overwhelming and also resulted in a lot of trial and error, losing out money, investing on the wrong products and implementing the wrong business strategies which simply just weren't working.

These business struggles are what has essentially inspired the writing of this book "**THE HAIR EMPIRE CEO**"- a comprehensive, practical and intensive step by step guide to helping anyone start and grow their own successful hair extension business from scratch.

This book is based on a combination of my personal experience running my online hair business over the years together with the aim of providing a simple, straight to the point, no fluff, and actionable step by step process to help you start your own hair extension company.

It is hoped that this book will be of use to both aspiring and existing hair business owners in helping them achieve long term business success.

FIRST THINGS FIRST

So now you have decided that you want to start your own hair extension business. Great Job! Starting your own business can be a very fun and rewarding experience although also challenging and demanding, but overall a profitable experience.

Starting a business in my opinion is like *"having a baby"*. It is exciting, emotional, changes your lifestyle, more responsibility, sleepless nights, and an almost non-existent social life, because you have to spend all day and night nursing that baby, looking after it until it grows into an adult and can function on its own. Overall it is an exciting, rewarding and profitable experience.

After all you are now building your own long term business lineage that could potentially leave an impact in generations to come.

However there is more to starting your own hair business than just coming up with an idea and making money out of it or having a burning desire to become your own boss. It will require several sacrifices, consistency and determination.

In fact be prepared to become your own manager, employee, accountant, marketer, sales person, advertisers, etc. especially if you are starting all on your own. Please bear in mind that this is not aimed at discouraging you, but preparing your mind-set for the big journey ahead.

Hence given the fact that starting a business requires a lot of commitment and sacrifices, you need to ensure you are mentally and physically prepared for the big journey ahead.

ABOUT HAIR TEXTURES

Now when it comes to hair, there are several different types of textures and variations that exist.

RAW HAIR

Raw hair is the most authentic and purest form of hair you will get. This hair contains no synthetic fibres and hasn't been processed (dyes, bleached, permed) in any shape of form. This type of hair is extremely scarce and also very expensive to obtain. Most raw hair will usually come directly from Indian temples where human hair is donated.

With raw hair the cuticles also come well aligned and are full to the ends - meaning the hair bundle doesn't start full at the top then thins outs at the end, thereby preventing tangling and matting.

Because the hair comes in its natural state, the luster tends not to be very shiny and may appear dull but natural. Raw hair also comes unwefted and hair may appear in different colours since it is coming from different donors.

Raw hair is the longest lasting grade of hair and can last up to 3 years if treated properly of course. Raw hair is extremely expensive to obtain, hence why a majority of people go for virgin hair.

VIRGIN HAIR

Virgin hair is naturally fine hair extensions that come with no synthetic hair fibres, comes from a single donor and is 100% human hair. Like raw hair, virgin hair comes in a natural luster and has no dyes, bleach, or colour with cuticles aligned in one direction - meaning the hair bundle doesn't start full at the top then thins outs at the thereby preventing matting and shedding. Unlike raw hair however, virgin hair is steam processed with water (not chemically processed) to achieve the different textures it comes in i.e. straight, body wave, deep wave, kinky curly etc. Virgin hair tends to last shorter than raw hair due to its processing i.e from 6 months to a year or 2 depending on how well the hair is treated and taken care of. With its different textures and natural luster, virgin hair is the most popular, affordable and easiest to obtain in the market and one which a majority of hair companies are currently selling.

REMY VS NON REMY HAIR

Under the Virgin Hair category falls the Remy and Non Remy Human Hair.

REMY HAIR

Remy Hair is the highest grade of virgin hair and most often you will see it called Virgin Remy Hair. This is 100% human hair, has a natural appearance and comes from a single donor with their cuticles aligned in the same direction, thereby preventing matting and shedding. Remy hair tends to be expensive (but not as expensive as raw hair). Remy hair is the most natural form of virgin hair and one which tends to last long with proper care and maintenance.

NON - REMY HAIR

Non Remy hair on the other hand is leftover hair that is collected from different places such as salon floors and temple floors. Because non Remy Hair is collected from different sources, it tends to go through a chemical acid processing to give it a natural look. As such it is difficult to tell by first look whether hair is Remy or Non Remy, as they all feel soft and have a nice luster to it.

Non Remy hair however has the cuticles unaligned meaning hair may appear thick at the top and then thin out towards the end. This means non Remy hair is likely to shed and become matted after one or two washes and doesn't usually tend to last any longer than a few months.

Non Remy hair is the cheapest form of human hair you will get. So if you ever see a hair company selling a hair bundle for something like $10, then there you have it - they are selling non Remy hair.

Some vendors' market non Remy hair as Remy hair - this is a very common occurrence on platforms such as Aliexpress. However, a good way to tell the difference is by taking a look at the cuticle alignment, the price (usually non Remy is the cheapest form of human hair you will get), and of course testing a few samples to see how well the hair holds up after one or two washes.

IS THE HAIR INDUSTRY REALLY SATURATED?

Some people say the hair industry is saturated and it's not worth getting into it. Now ask yourself this question, if the founder of McDonalds had thought, "Wait a minute there is already a KFC and other hosts of fast food restaurants opening" back in the 1950's then there will be no McDonalds today.

Likewise there will be no Apple, Samsung, and all the other host of smartphone companies out there if one of the founders said "oh wait, the phone industry is saturated".

I mean what industry isn't saturated though?

The point here is, although it may seem like there are many people selling hair, one thing to remember is that there is also billions of dollars being spent on hair, with demand increasing and the industry getting even bigger. In my opinion, competition is a good thing - because it's an indication that something is working, hence why people are tapping into that industry.

There is money - I mean plenty of money to be made out here and even if your business could tap into just a little 1% of that billion dollar pie, you could be making 10,000,000 - and that's just a tiny chunk of the industry.

So although it seems like everyone around your neighbourhood is selling hair, trust me there isn't a billion hair companies out there catering to every single individual in need of hair. This means demand is still greater than supply which is a good thing for you and therefore a potential for you to start you own hair business.

Secondly people have choices and will prefer to shop from one brand over the other. e.g. KFC over McDonalds, Apple over Samsung etc. People have preferences and you just will never know the endless benefits your brand could bring people out there - unless of course you get started.

WHERE DOES HUMAN HAIR REALLY COME FROM?

You have probably heard about all types of hair from Brazilian, Malaysian, Peruvian, Russian, Indian, hair etc. The truth is, all this human hair really comes from temples in India.

So Indian women donate their hair in Hindu temples as part of their culture and tradition. This hair is then collected, exported to China where it is cleaned, treated and wefted into extensions that can be usable.

Hair doesn't come from Brazil, Malaysia, Peru, Russia, but the hair is named after the wave pattern & texture of the hair. e.g Brazilian hair will be the wave pattern in which Brazilian women wear their hair, etc. makes sense now?

The truth is, all these big hair companies source their hair from **India & China**. India donates the hair, and this hair is then transformed into a wearable form in most cases in China.

The Chinese are responsible for treating, wefting this hair and turning them into wearable conditions hence why majority of hair comes from China.

This is exactly why so many hair companies are opening these days without even a warehouse. They source the hair from China in a ready to use condition, re brand it with their business name and resell it to customers.

And yes this is perfectly OK! Consumers need this hair and companies play the role of bringing this product to the target market who need this hair. And guess what? The market is indeed booming.

This is just to give you the reality of where human hair really comes from and how you too could benefit as a part of this billion dollar industry.

One thing to note however is that; all human hair will NOT be the same. Now hair donated by a young person will usually look and feel healthier than hair donated by the elderly women. This is simply because hair donated by the older have gone through longer years, hair has been dyed, treated and undergone different procedures prior to being donated to the temples. Hair from the young however haven't been through a lot of this and will therefore be a lot more durable and healthy.

Secondly hair donated by Sandra will be different from hair donated by Tracy because guess what? They care for their hair differently.

Overall, the hair industry is a gamble and the secret to a successful hair business is down to;

"FINDING THE RIGHT HAIR VENDORS"

This is something we will talk about in more detail in another section. But in the meantime, let's explore other vital topics.

AVOID THESE MISTAKES WHEN STARTING YOUR HAIR BUSINESS

Now that we have explored some of the key basics to getting your hair company up and running, there are also a few important things you need to be wary of when starting your hair business.

Buying Too Much Inventory

Inventory is one of those things that can either make or break your hair business. Now unlike many other products out there, buying hair wholesale is expensive to say the least. And guess what? Most vendors require you to buy in **BULK**.

Inventory is essentially the core to the success of your hair business and where most of your money will be tied up on. So when starting out, it is extremely important to not invest too much money on inventory too early on in your business. Remember you are still an extremely new brand and not so many people know about your brand just yet.

If you go ahead and invest thousands of dollars on hundreds of units, not only will you need to find space to store all that inventory but you also risk your products not selling and all your money being tied up in stock. We will talk about avoiding this problem using a powerful inventory sourcing strategy which is discussed in more detail later on in this book.

Expecting to Get Rich Overnight

One reason most entrepreneurs and business owners fail is simply because they quit too early on in their business journey. They start a business today and expect to start making money as soon as possible which is simply unrealistic and unattainable in most cases. What you need to focus on initially is creating that brand awareness and building a relationship with your clients as a trusted brand. Once people start to discover your brand and trust you, there are likely to start purchasing from you in the long run. It might take a day, a week, a month and even years to see any results, but this will all depend on how well you chose to run your business and mostly how consistent and patient you are during that journey. So do not quit your job just yet, keep working on that business and it will eventually pay off.

Making Excuses

One reason most businesses never succeed is simply because of the excuses. I've received so many emails and messages from clients constantly telling me they want to start a business but lack the money, don't have time, or have other commitments, etc. What I call this is Excuses! If the CEO's of successful multi-billion dollar companies made excuses each time they had a business idea, there will be no business out here today. I started my online clothing brands FashVie with less than £300 and whilst working full time. Yes that's right!

I self-taught myself on how to create my own website. It took me weeks and even months of trial and testing but thanks to Google, Youtube and books, I was able to create my first ever ecommerce website. I then decided to use dropshipping as an inventory sourcing approach which also saved me thousands on wholesale inventory.

If money is a problem, why not find ways to save money through cutting back on some expenses you don't need, taking some extra shifts at work, or even borrowing from family and friends? Instead of making excuses as to why you can't start your business just yet, why not invest that time finding other ways to work around what you have right now and make the most of it? You see, there really is nothing stopping you from getting started but yourself.

STARTING ONLINE VS OFFLINE

So should you start your hair business online or offline?

One of the big questions most people tend to have is deciding on whether to start their hair business online or to start a brick and mortar store offline. Now the answer to that will be dependent on a number of factors listed below;

Finance

Financially it is obviously more expensive to open a brick and mortar or traditional offline store. Firstly you need to think about the cost of premises, stationery, inventory, perhaps paying some staff, etc.

As you can imagine, it could cost you thousands of pounds or dollars to launch such a business. However, with an online store, you only need to worry about the cost of getting your website up and running, getting some inventory and you are pretty much good to go.

And since you are based online, you don't need to hold too much inventory is required in comparison to a brick and mortar store which usually needs to be fully stocked to appeal to customers.

Customer Reach

With a brick and mortar or offline store, you are only able to reach out to customers in your local and geographical area who pop into your store to shop. However, with an online store, you are not only limiting yourself to your city but can reach out to customers worldwide – remember you are on the World Wide Web.

In fact recently, there has been an influx of offline brick and mortar stores now opening online stores in order to appeal to a wider audience with some reporting more sales online than offline.

Flexibility

Another value of starting an online hair business versus an offline one is the flexibility to run that business and make money from it whilst still working on your full time or part time job, studying or focusing on other life commitments. You are not required to make any drastic changes to your lifestyle to operate and run an online store. With an offline store however, you need to be physically present in the store to attend to customers and make any money. If you close that business, you don't make any sales (*unless of course you are equally trading online*).

Tangibility

One reason most people tend to opt for offline stores over online ones is due to the tangibility factor. Some customers' still prefer to see, feel, touch and try on products prior to buying them – something offline stores offer.

However, with an online hair business this option is unavailable which can put some people off buying hair from you. Nevertheless with some good product images, video blurbs and detailed item descriptions, most people tend to be ok with shopping online which is still proving a very popular option.

Personally I do not own a brick and mortar offline store at the moment as my business is doing pretty well online and I do not see the point of incurring additional expenses offline. Moreover so many offline stores are now closing down (*just read the news or look around you*) every single day due to competition from online counterparts which again could indicate a red flag trying to open an offline hair store.

So in conclusion, I will recommend you start online to test the waters, then once your business picks up or if you have the finances and resources available, you could then also open an offline store. It's really a personal decision and up to you which option resonates best with you.

Remember pop up shops and showrooms are also cheaper alternatives if you want to sell your products offline.

YOUR SUCCESS STRATEGY

Planning your success strategy is extremely vital when starting your hair company. Think of your success strategy as a roadmap to your overall business success. Your success strategy comprises of three key areas namely; *your mission, your vision and your strategy.*

MISSION

Your mission is the *"core message of your brand"*. What do you want to be known as? What do you want your brand to represent? What do you want people to remember your hair business as? Start brainstorming on the core message of your online hair company and what you want it to represent and note this down in your worksheet.

Remember it doesn't have to be perfect at this stage as you can always revisit this and change as you progress with your business.

VISION

Your vision refers to the long term goals for your business. This is the part where you visualise more long term. Where do you see your brand in the next 3-6 months, 1-3 years, etc.? I want you to really get your thinking caps on and start visualising and writing down where you want your brand to be in the next few months and years to come. It may sound crazy and unattainable right now, but that's the whole idea! Just write those crazy thoughts down. You will soon look back and wonder why you ever thought it was a crazy idea.

STRATEGIC OBJECTIVES

Your strategic objectives are basically your plan of action, to do list, what steps you intend to take to achieve that mission and long term vision. Purchasing this book is already one strategy since you are taking action towards achieving that long term vision of starting your own hair company.

Start brainstorming on what you want to achieve by the end of each month then see whether you need to create a new success strategy or update your existing one if not much has changed.

Remember your strategic objectives are likely to change along the way, just make sure you are in tune with them.

NICHE/BUSINESS IDEA

Now that you have decided to start your own hair company, one of the most important first steps to starting your hair company is identifying a niche or market you want to focus on. Overall the best inspirations and motivations should come from things you love and personally enjoy, from personal experience, and most of all something you have a passion for.

Hopefully by now you fully understand the different hair textures and have an idea with regards to which one you are most likely interested in.

There are a few areas in the hair extensions industry you could specialise in. So you might want to decide at this stage what area you think you would enjoy running your business on.

Do you want to focus on selling;

- ❖ **Clip in Extensions**
- ❖ **Human Hair Wigs (full Lace front Wigs, U part Wigs?**
- ❖ **Custom made wigs**
- ❖ **Virgin Remy Human Hair**
- ❖ **Virgin Non- Remy Human Hair**

- ❖ Raw Human Hair
- ❖ Fusion/Bonded Tape in hair
- ❖ Synthetic Hair
- ❖ Braiding and Crocheting

To help determine what niche you could focus on, a few questions you could ask yourself are;

- ☐ *What inspired you to want to start your own hair company?*
- ☐ *What type of hairstyles do you currently wear yourself the most?*
- ☐ *Have you seen other hair companies and thought you could start one better than that?*
- ☐ *Or maybe you are just passionate about hair and would love to become your own boss?*
- ☐ *Do people compliment your hair all the time? Which styles in particular?*
- ☐ *Which type of products from the list above do you tend to spend MOST of your money on, on a*

weekly, monthly basis? Now that might just be the niche you should focus on. Something you already use and have a passion for right?

Do not try to be broad when selecting a niche by trying to sell everything because, not only will your customers find this confusing, but it will also be difficult for you to identify your target market. **After all you are not a shopping mall!**

What type of hair extensions do you currently wear yourself? What type of hair extensions are you most interested in? So think about that and this should give you a great idea on which part to focus on.

Once you identify your niche, it will be easier in the long run to identify and sell to your ideal customer. e.g a wig company won't appeal to people who are more interested in crocheting or braids.

And don't feel like you are missing out on anything by not selling everything out there in your store. Trust me, focusing on a target group of people will help a great deal with the launching of your hair business which you will discover later on in this book.

Whichever decision you make at this stage will have a long term impact on your overall business strategy so please take your time and brainstorm properly.

Got an idea now? Great let's move onto the next step.

YOUR MARKETING MIX

Now we have some ideas with regards to what type of hair we want to sell, it's time to dive deeper into how you plan to execute your online hair company through looking into the Marketing Mix which comprises of the 4P's, **product, price, place and promotion** as identified by Michael Porter. For service based businesses, this could also include the three other; *people, processes and physical evidence.* However we will be focusing on the 4P's which are the most relevant to your online hair business.

Product/Service – A product is an offer that meets a need in the market. This can be a physical object or a service introduced into the market to satisfy the desire or need after purchase and use or consumption. So for your hair company, *what type of hair products (niche) do you plan on selling?*

Price – The price is the amount of money the consumer will spend in order to acquire the product or service or how you plan to monetise your business. So for your hair business, *how do you plan to price your products and make money from your hair business?*

Place – The place refers to the where you plan to sell the products such as; distribution channels, location, distribution networks, assortment, locations, availability, transport, logistics. *So where do you plan to sell your hair products or services? Is it through your own website, social media, a* *showroom, direct marketing or an external platform?*

Promotion – This refers to what channels you plan to use to communicate your products or services to your customers such as advertising, marketing, sponsorships, etc. This could be through flyer distributions, referrals (word of mouth), social media marketing, word of mouth influencers, networking events, etc? *How do you plan to advertise or reach out to your customers?*

So why not grab a pen and paper right now, and start brainstorming on and creating the 4 P'S for your own online hair company.

What types of hair products do you want to sell, approximately how much will it cost to buy and sell them, where do you plan to sell them and how do you plan on promoting your brand?

You may not have all this information yet, however try to come up with some rough estimates for now.

Part 2

BUSINESS REGISTRATION & LEGAL

CHOOSING A BUSINESS NAME

Now we have an idea and have also conducted some research, the next step is coming up with a business name. At this stage you might want to start thinking about what to call your hair business. It should be something straight to the point that immediately tells people what it is you do. It should also reflect on who you are especially if selling services.

The business name is the first thing that any potential buyer is going to notice and in this respect is what is likely to draw people's attention and get them curious. You might have the best idea in the world but if people are looking elsewhere because your competitors name 'looks' more attractive then no-one will ever know.

Therefore, it's essential that you strike the right tone with your business' name. Get creative; ask people around you what they think of it. Note down a list of different names and pick which one suits you best. Don't make it too long or too short.

Keep it memorable and straight to the point! For example, some people prefer having their names linked to their brand. So if your name is Sandra and you have decided to start your own hair company, you could call it something like; sandras lengths, sandrashair, sandra extensions, etc.

Or you could come up with something that doesn't have your name linked to it such as; fabhairs.com, etc. Once you come up with a name, you also want to make sure that the name isn't already registered or trademarked by someone else, the domain name isn't already registered, and it isn't already being used on other social media pages. The last thing you want is your customers landing on other people's businesses. Or worst still, invest on a name that is already taken by someone else.

You can check that your domain name isn't already registered at: **NameCheap.com**

You can check that your business name isn't registered at:

https://www.informdirect.co.uk/company-format ions/form-company-byshr/

https://beta.companieshouse.gov.uk/company-na me-availability

https://www.sec.gov/edgar/searchedgar/compan ysearch.html

TRADEMARKS & COPYRIGHT

Trademarking your name is another important aspect of your business. Although it is not a requirement to do this as soon as possible, it is something to definitely look into as you proceed with your business launch. Trademarking your business name gives you full ownership of that name and the legal right to sue anyone who tries to use your business name for whatever purposes.

Once you come up with a name, you also want to make sure that the name isn't already trademarked by someone else to avoid any copyright issues. The last thing you want is to end up in a legal battle with another company for using their business name. You can check with the Intellectual Property Office to ensure that the name isn't already taken. If based in the UK, you can check this at

https://www.gov.uk/search-for-trademark If based in the USA you can check your trademark name at:

https://www.uspto.gov/trademarks-application-process/search-trademark-database#heading-1

It currently costs £170 as at 2019 to register a trademark in the UK and can be done at: https://www.gov.uk/how-to-register-a-trade-mark. This process is usually lengthy and sometimes you might need to get a trademark lawyer.

For those based in the USA, please consult the IRS website at https://www.irs.gov as trademark registrations differ with each state. For all other countries, please consult with your relevant governmental boards. If your business name isn't showing up as trademarked, then you are good to go.

CHOOSING A BUSINESS STRUCTURE

Now we have a business name, it is time to start looking into the different business structures. When it comes to selecting a business structure, there are a variety of options you can choose from, all dependent on how you plan to operate.

Sole Proprietorship/Sole Trader – This is the easiest way to register your business and is ideal if you plan to run your business alone. There is less paperwork involved in getting registered, all the profits earned are yours, however you are also liable for any debts - meaning if you took a loan from the bank and your business went bankrupt, then your personal assets could be liable for repossession by the bank. You are also required to register for VAT (if based in the UK) depending on whether or not your annual sales are expected to reach a threshold of £85,000 (HMRC, 2018).

So if you believe your sales for the first year will be less than £85,000, then there's no need to register for VAT however you still have the option to voluntarily register.

Partnership - This is ideal for a business being run by two people. In a partnership, you and your partner (or partners) personally share responsibility for your business and are both liable for any debts. This includes: any losses your business makes, bills for things you buy for your business, like stock or equipment. Partners share the business's profits, and each partner pays tax on their share. (HMRC, 2018). The VAT rules again are similar to the above.

Private Limited Company or LLC- This is ideal for those who plan on not just running the business themselves but having other shareholders and stakeholders involved. For example if you are thinking about obtaining funding from investors or lenders (who usually require a percentage of your company in return), or plan to hire employees in the future, then it's probably best to register as a limited company.

As a company you can also pay yourself dividends which are usually not taxed. You must appoint people to run the company (called 'directors') and register (or 'incorporate') it with Companies House (UK) or the IRS (USA).

As a director of the company, you can also become an employee. This means that personal income and business income are separate when it comes to paying tax. You will also be required to pay Corporation tax every end of the year and

VAT quarterly if you register for it and PAYE if you plan to hire employee.

As a limited company you are separate from your business, meaning any debts incurred by the business do not directly affect your own personal assets. You can either register your company yourself, or hire an accountant or solicitor to help. It cost £12 as of April 2018, and usually requires more paperwork completion to be fully incorporated.

PLEASE NOTE: *If you are based outside the UK, then check with your relevant local government on the company registration process. For US based readers please check with* *https://www.irs.gov*

REGISTERING YOUR BUSINESS

Now you are getting close to your big launch, it's probably a good idea to start looking into getting your business registered. You can register your business either as a sole proprietorship, partnership or Ltd company (LLC). Below are the different platforms you can look into registering with for different countries.

FOR UNITED STATES

SOLE TRADER OR PARTNERSHIP

If you are using your REAL name as your business name, then there is no need to register. However if using a fictitious business name or anything other than your real name as your business name, then you need to file a DBA (Doing Business As) at:

https://www.legalzoom.com/business/business-formation/dba-overview.html

ALL OTHER COMPANY TYPES - If registering as an LLC or Corp, you MUST register your business. More information on getting started can be found at:

https://www.legalzoom.com/business/business-formation/llc-overview.html

FOR UNITED KINGDOM

SOLE TRADER OR PARTNERSHIP

Register as Self Employed, whether using a fictitious name or your REAL name at:

https://www.gov.uk/log-in-file-self-assessment-tax-return/register-if-youre-self-employed

ALL OTHER COMPANY TYPES

If registering as an ltd or Plc you MUST register your business with Companies House at:

https://www.gov.uk/topic/company-registration-filing/starting-company

FOR OTHER COUNTRIES, PLEASE CONSULT YOUR RELEVANT STATE OR LOCAL GOVERNMENT FOR MORE INFORMATION.

PLEASE NOTE: This information is valid at the time of publication and may be subject to changes moving forward. Always double check with your relevant governmental websites or legal adviser for any latest changes.

SELLER'S PERMITS

A seller's permit is also known as a sales tax license, wholesale license, resale license, sales tax certification and retail license. There appears to be a little confusion around obtaining seller's permit and whether or not you need one for your hair business.

As a rule of thumb, if you plan on buying products wholesale and reselling or, are physically handling products you sell (e.g. through making your own products) then a seller's permit is required. A sellers permit is also required if you plan on charging or collecting sales tax on your products. In the UK this is equivalent to a VAT registration number.

If you plan on drop shipping, then obtaining a seller's permit may be optional especially given the fact that you are not physically buying, reselling and handling any shipment yourself.

However do bear in mind that, seller's permits laws tend to differ for each country and state and its best to check with your local state or government to establish what each process involves in more detail.

So essentially, if you plan on buying and reselling, physically handling products or plan on charging sales tax on your products, then a sellers permit or VAT registration number is required by law.

You can check with the IRS (USA) or Gov.uk (UK) to find out more information on registering for a sellers' permit or a VAT number.

YOUR EIN NUMBER

An EIN number also refers to an **Employer Identification Number**. This is the terminology commonly used in the United States of America. In the UK this is similar to the **PAYE (Pay as You Earn)** Reference number.

An EIN number is usually required for businesses that plan on hiring and paying staff. So if you are a sole trader working alone with no employee, then an EIN number is usually not required, instead you can use you social security number. If you plan on registering your business as an LLC or hiring staff, then you can register for an EIN at: https://www.irs.gov/businesses/small-businesses

-self-employed/do-you-need-an-ein

Please note that, most times wholesalers may request for an EIN number in addition to a sellers permit before you can buy from them, so endeavour to check this with your wholesalers.

The same rule applies to those in the United Kingdom. So if you are a sole trader working alone with no employees, then usually a PAYE Reference is not required. However if you plan on hiring staff, then you can register for a PAYE Reference   at: https://www.gov.uk/register-employer

DISCLAIMER: Always double check with your relevant governmental websites or legal adviser for any latest changes to these rules.

BUSINESS INSURANCE

No matter how successful your business seems, accidents do occur at times we do not expect. Getting business insurance for your hair business is necessary for your own protection and benefit.

Business insurance will also depend on the nature of your business as it is a legal requirement for some businesses to have business insurance. For example, professional indemnity insurance is required if you offer professional services. If working from home, also check that your home insurance policy covers you to work from home.

Even if you have a successful business, disaster could strike at any moment and force you to shut your doors. Although it might seem tempting to cut costs by forgoing insurance, it is a good idea to look into a business insurance policy.

There are a lot of cheap business insurance policies out there starting from as little as £5 per month.

You can visit www.moneysupermarket.com or www.gocompare.com to compare different insurance providers, do your research right, read reviews others have left before purchasing any type of insurance policy.

Part 3

YOUR BUSINESS FINANCES

FUNDING YOUR BUSINESS

Now you are ready to start your hair company, there are several options you could look into to help with the financing of your new business venture. Now depending on the inventory sourcing options you choose to go for and how you plan to run your business, you may or may not require any external funding.

As previously mentioned, one of the key benefits of starting an online hair business versus a traditional brick and mortar store is the low start-up costs and capital required. However, if you need help financing your business, then there are so many different ways of financing a business including loans, grants, overdrafts, leasing, etc.

PERSONAL FINANCING

The easiest form of funding to procure is your existing money. A large number of business owners secure part of business funding from their wallet.

After all, it is one of the common places to begin with the venture. Available options include personal savings, money acquired from credit cards, friends and family, insurance policies and home equity.

CROWDFUNDING

Crowd funding is another superb option for online fundraising. It brings a community of investors, start-ups, entrepreneurs and businesses together and let them meet each other to accomplish their objectives. There are many crowdfunding websites available on the internet that lets you promote your promising ideas and materialize them in a better way. However, the drawback of these platforms is high transaction costs that can range from 5% to 10% of the total amount raised. Visit http://www.ukcfa.org.uk/, www.gofundme.com for great platforms to get started.

BUSINESS LOANS

If you are looking for a way to acquire sufficient amount of money to fund your business, small business loans can provide you with the same at comparatively low rate of interest. However, if you make up your mind to go with this option, ensure to seek help from a community lender or credit union rather than nationwide bank since the chances of approval of your application are more with them.

BUSINESS BANK ACCOUNT

Most people tend to use their personal bank accounts for business. But should you really open a business bank account? While it may be tempting to start your new business venture without looking at the need for a bank account dedicated to your business activity, this might not be the smartest of choice.

As your business grows and expands, it's extremely important to separate your business finances from your personal, day-to-day living. Not only is this important to keep proper track of your finances and manageable, having a business account where customers can pay you via direct debit, cheques, seems very professional.

While many business current accounts available charge you for their services, there are others that waive the charge as long as you pay in more than a certain amount each month.

Make sure that you shop around for the best options and you can take advantage of the best deals – don't assume that your personal banking provider will be the smartest choice for business use.

And remember if you find it difficult opening a business account, you can always open another personal account but use it for business purposes - except of course it won't come with some of the benefits offered by a business account.

ACCOUNTING & TAXES

The moment people hear the word accounting or taxes, they start regretting why they even started a business. I know exactly what you are thinking right now;

I hate anything to do with numbers. I can't even afford an accountant, how do you expect me to do this? Do I really need an accountant at this stage?

Now this is an area I'm really passionate about because my first ever business was a bookkeeping business.

During that time, I encountered different types of clients, from the ones who wrote their finances on pen and paper to the ones who didn't even keep their receipts, invoices etc.

The message here is, do not wait until your business starts making sales before you start keeping track of your books.

The little expenses you have already spent on such as; web design, web hosting, domain name, laptop, company registration fees, business insurance, inventory, even this book, and all those little spends are already business expenses you should be keeping track of.

Now some of you might be lucky to have family, friends that can do your accounts for you, however for others this may not be the case. If you are looking for an easy and affordable way to keep track of your day to day finances, then you can save yourself the costs by using Ms Excel Bookkeeping spreadsheets such as those offered by **No Hassle Accounting** at www.nohassleaccounting.com, or alternatively hire a bookkeeper if you can afford to.

With this bookkeeping software, you can manage your day to day finances, track your cash flow and know exactly how well your business is performing.

You can then hire an accountant *(if required)* for the more complicated tasks such as year-end tax returns and company accounts especially if you run a Ltd or LLC Company.

PAYING YOURSELF AS A BUSINESS OWNER

Before you begin paying yourself a salary from your business, you need to ensure that your business is making a substantial amount of profit (**not revenue**). Do not confuse profit for revenue. Profit is what is left over after all expenses have been deducted and cleared. Revenue on the other hand comes from sales you have received from your customers prior to any deductions.

For example say you are selling a hair bundle for $100 and a customer buys that hair at $100, then $100 essentially is your **Revenue or Sales**. For each item you sell, there are a few direct costs that come from the acquisition, packaging and shipping of that product which all need to be deducted from this revenue before you can boast of a profit.

Say for example the cost of that hair was $30, then PayPal or Stripe deducted fees of $2, you then needed to package and ship that product to your customers which is also included in the cost of stationery (business cards, flyers, and printing costs), etc. So assuming your total expenses were $35, then your **profit will be $65** ($100 - $35). Therefore, you can then only pay yourself from this $65 profit leftover and **NOT** the $100.

When just starting out your hair business, it is usually a good idea to avoid paying yourself too soon, but rather reinvest your profits back into your business until it gains stability.

Once your business starts consistently generating profits that are equivalent to 1.5 – 2 times the cost of your living expenses, you can then start paying yourself.

For example, if you need $1000 to survive each month, then you might want to wait till your business is generating profits between $1500-$2000 first. So calculate your cost of living each month, then multiply that by 1.5 or 2.

If your business is generating that final amount in **PROFIT**, then you could start thinking about paying yourself a monthly salary. Your monthly salary should equal your living expenses, and the rest of the money put back into your business. Remember you can always pay yourself an additional bonus if business is moving even better than anticipated.

So in conclusion, only pay yourself once a business is generating a profit of at least 1.5 - 2 times your living expenses, then only pay yourself the equivalent of what you spend or need to survive each month.

Here's a little summary;

If Business profits for the month = $1500 - $2000

And Your Living Expenses = $1000

You Should Pay Yourself Living Expenses = $1000

Then Put back in Business = $500 - $1000

PLEASE NOTE: Again these figures are just a recommendation based on what has worked best for me and not a requirement to stick to these amounts. Please go with what works best for you.

Part 4

INVENTORY & SUPPLIERS

HOW TO SOURCE INVENTORY

One of the most important steps in starting a hair business is deciding on how and what type of hair to source for your business. There are two key ways to source inventory for your hair business.

BUY WHOLESALE

This is a very popular method of sourcing inventory which usually involves buying hair in bulk at a low price from a supplier, then reselling it at a higher price to your customers. You are responsible for all the inventory management, packaging, shipping, branding, etc. This is usually pretty expensive especially considering how much stock you need to purchase in advance and upfront financial commitments.

DROPSHIPPING

This involves selling products on your website with no need to purchase any inventory in advance. Simply find a dropshipping supplier, start selling their products on your website (at a higher retail price), when a customer buys from you, you pass their shipping details to the supplier (keeping the profit) and the supplier deals with the packaging and shipping of products directly to them. This is of course our most preferred option for sourcing inventory as it means you can start your hair business with little to no money **(more on this is discussed later).** In the next sections we will be focusing more in-depth on sourcing your hair through buying wholesale and most importantly dropshipping which is my most recommended option when just starting out.

WHERE TO FIND WHOLESALE HAIR SUPPLIERS

Wholesale involves buying products at a low cost from wholesale suppliers, and then reselling them at a higher mark-up price to your customers. This is a great option for those who have capital to invest upfront on inventory. However be aware that most wholesale suppliers expect you to buy products in bulk which could be extremely costly.

When it comes to buying hair wholesale, unless you have your own hair factory where you weft, process and treat the hair into a wearable condition, your best option will be to either travel to India or China to source those vendors.

You could either book a flight to these countries then find the temples and factories yourself (very expensive option), or find wholesale vendors who already sell this hair and have a good track record of delivering good quality hair (easiest option).

One of the biggest platforms to find wholesale hair vendors is none other than www.alibaba.com. When sourcing vendors from Alibaba, the key things to look out for are;

Business Duration

Check how long they have been in business for. This will tell you how legit and reliable they are. I will be weary using any suppliers who are under 3 years old simply because if a business can survive its first three years, then it means they are probably doing something right. This is however not to say that suppliers under 3 years old are bad or every supplier 3 years and older is automatically perfect.

Location

Alibaba also allows you to filter results by location. So for example you can type human hair, then select what locations you want the vendors to come from as shown below;

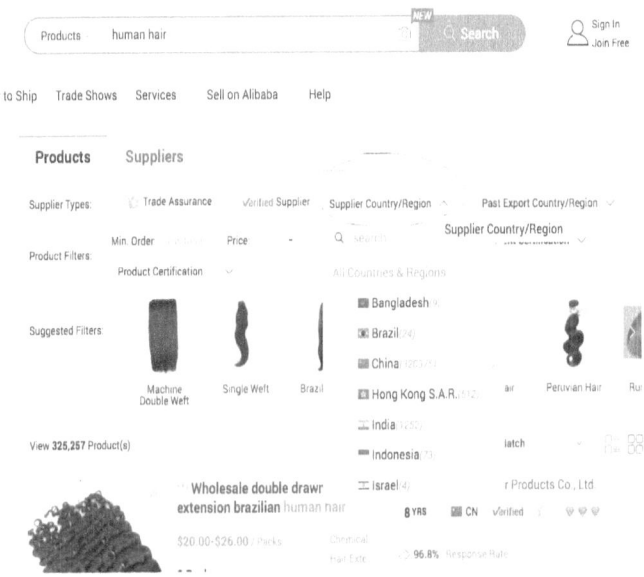

However this usually tends to limit your search results and supplier options to almost no results.

Number of Units Shipped Out

Check how many transactions they have shipped out over the last few months. The good thing about Alibaba is that it publicly shows you all that data. This will also be a good indication on whether or not they are reliable.

Reviews

Reviews are extremely essential when sourcing wholesale vendors for your hair business. Another good thing about Alibaba is that it displays all the reviews left by previous buyers on each of the vendors. However beware of fake reviews.

Trade Assurance

When looking for vendors on Alibaba, always make sure that they hold trade assurance. This means if the supplier sends out a product which doesn't match the quality they advertised, you can easily dispute that transaction and a refund could be issued.

You can find out my ticking on Trade Assurance during your search, and it should only display vendors who hold one.

Response Rate

Again this is data that is provided to you by Alibaba. You can see exactly how fast each individual supplier responds to queries which can be a massive bonus when it comes to doing business with them.

So my recommendations when using alibaba.com is to search for the keywords as appropriate e.g. "human hair"

Next tick the boxes that state **"Trade Assurance"** and **"Verified Suppliers"**.

This should filter your results by bringing up the best recommended suppliers. You can then contact the suppliers to find out if they offer samples, etc. I would recommend you test out samples before you commit to a big bulk wholesale purchase.

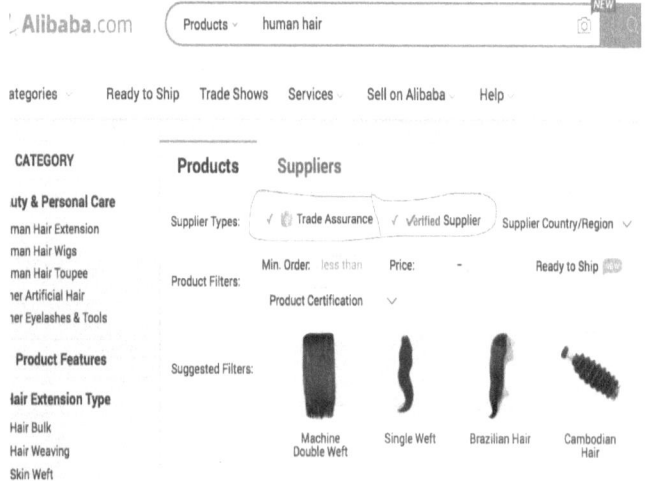

Another great platform you could use to find wholesale suppliers is on Instagram – believe it or not. If you go on Instagram and do a hashtag search on the words **#wholesalehair**, it will bring up different accounts of sellers currently selling wholesale hair. It also brings you other recommendations of other keywords you could look out for as shown below;

Remember to always do your due diligence on any suppliers you decide to us.

Another great platform you could look into for wholesale hair suppliers and vendors is; www.dhgate.com.

BONUS LIST OF HAIR SUPPLIERS

Meanwhile, I have put together a FREE bonus list of some wholesale hair vendors for you below;

https://www.bigloveindianhair.com/
https://www.dhwarak.com/
https://www.sgihair.com/
https://www.jaipurhair.com/
https://www.klaiyihair.com/
https://www.favirginhair.com/
https://www.kabeilu.com/
https://www.perfectlocks.com/
https://jcwholesalevirginhair.com/
https://www.eapollowholesale.co.uk/
https://www.virginhairvendor.com/

For access to even more human hair, wigs and lashes vendors, please visit www.sellpire.com

DISCLAIMER: Always do your own research on any vendors you decide to use, better still order some samples and test out first, and undertake your own due diligence

HOW TO START A HAIR BUSINESS WITH LITTLE TO NO MONEY

For those who aren't familiar with the term, drop shipping - it's a technique whereby the retailer or seller (you) does not keep any goods in stock. Instead when a customer buys from you, you then transfer the customer orders and shipment details to the supplier who then ships the goods directly to the customer.

With dropshipping you do not need to handle any inventory whatsoever and hence no need to buy stock in advance. Is like selling stock you don't even own. That's how dropshipping works.

In a retail businesses, the majority of retailers make their profit on the difference between the wholesale and retail price but some retailers earn an agreed percentage of the sales in commission, paid by the wholesaler to the retailer. With dropshipping you sell a product on behalf of the wholesaler, send the customer information to the wholesaler who then distributes the product directly to the customer while you keep the profits. So you are like the bridge between the supplier and customer - except you do not need to buy or hold any inventory in advance as with the case of wholesale.

If you are interested in starting a hair business, but don't have a lot of money to invest in wholesale hair just yet, or perhaps you are still looking to test the waters to see if the hair business is for you or before investing big, then **dropshipping is the answer**.

Now unlike many other products out there, buying hair is expensive to say the least. On average, a 10 inch bundle at wholesale price will cost you around $30 for good quality hair. Now let's do some quick maths; If you are buying at the minimum 10 bundles of each length, then:

10 inches @ $30 per piece X 10 = $300

12 inches@ $35 per piece X 10 = $350

14 inches @ $40 per piece X 10 = $400

16 inches @ $45 per piece X 10 = $450

18 inches @ $50 per piece X 10 = $500

20 inches @ $55 per piece X 10 = $550

22 inches @ $60 per piece X 10 = $600

24 inches @ $65 per piece X 10 = $650

26 inches @ $70 per piece X 10 = $700

Total = $4200.

And do bear in mind this is just for one hair bundle in one curl pattern. Now you have to think about getting that in straight, body wave and curly patterns.

Now assuming you wanted to stick to just selling Straight, Body wave and Curly, then that's $4200 X 3 = **$12600**.

So as you can see, you will be needing on average **a minimum of $10,000** just for inventory - and again that's an average estimate for a very small hair business.

Most likely you will spend more than this as most often, suppliers require you to purchase minimum orders of more than 10 units - with some in the range of 100's as minimum orders per piece.

So how then do you start a hair company with little to no money?

Well as previously highlighted, dropshipping is the best and only way around this. Believe it or not most of those big hair companies you currently buy hair from are using a dropshipping business model.

Ever wondered how and why it takes some USA based hair companies 7-10 days to ship hair to you who is also based in the USA?

Well the answer is simple! They are using a dropshipping business model and the products are coming directly from their dropshipping supplier most likely from China.

This is an extremely smart business strategy because they don't risk any money buying too much inventory that may not sell. They simply sell those products whilst the supplier handles all the shipping and fulfilment for them.

And some of these hair companies have showrooms, where they only display a few hair samples and nothing more. Again because they are using a dropshipping business model.

Some dropshipping vendors also offer custom and private labelling, meaning they actually ship out these products with those brands information i.e. flyers, business cards, packaging making it even harder for customers to spot things.

With drop shipping you have the flexibility to sell these products under your own business name with your own set prices. And you can select what products you want to sell and list them on your own website.

Now let's do a little test.

Go on Instagram right now and check out some of the big hair companies you currently follow or even shop from in the USA, UK or wherever you are based. Now visit their websites and take a look at their shipping policies. I can guarantee you that most of their shipping times state 5 -7 or 7-15 business days. This is a business model that I used for about a year when I started my hair company Yes Weave before eventually stocking our own inventory when sales started to pick up and our dropshipping and distribution program launched.

So where do you find Dropshipping Hair Suppliers?

Most wholesale vendors usually tend to offer a dropshipping service too. But in most cases, you will need to contact them to find out if they do, as some still don't even understand what dropshipping is.

Secondly some dropshipping companies require you to be a registered business and spend at least $500 a month to remain a dropshipper.

But you need to be very careful when picking a dropshipper because a majority of them end up charging people to become dropshippers and never delivering what they claim. Unless a dropshipping supplier is offering you additional or extra services such as; web design, private labelling, custom packaging or any additional services other than just using them as a dropshipper, I wouldn't recommend you use them as a dropshipper.

So if any dropshipping supplier out there is charging you extra, make sure they are offering something extra.

Some Good News for You

The good news for you reading this book right now is that, Yes Weave currently offers a dropshipping program through our distributor program which currently has thousands of members. We have created a platform that allows you to drop ship human hair weaves, closures, frontals and wigs.

And our distributor prices come at low wholesale costs thereby allowing you to charge your own high prices whilst we deal with all the hard-work of shipping, packaging and processing your orders for you.

Furthermore, all the products are shipped unlabelled and with no invoice attached meaning your customers will never know the hair came from us, or how much you paid us.

And included in our Distributor Business starter kit is;

- ❖ Access to your own pre-designed website, preloaded with products ready to sell
- ❖ We hold the inventory for you - so you don't need to invest thousands of dollars on wholesale hair
- ❖ FREE Samples to test out the hair
- ❖ Marketing Training courses and eBooks
- ❖ FREE Accounts Software to keep track of Your Finances
- ❖ FREE Web Hosting
- ❖ Business Flyers included

And everything you need to start your own hair company.

All of it comes at a one off annual price starting from just of **$199 ($16pm).** Not bad for an all in one hair business starter kit right. Well if you compare it to $10,000 dollars you will need to spend on wholesale inventory if you decide to buy your own inventory, then another couple of thousands to pay someone to design your website, then another investment on marketing, etc, then I think it's fair to say that the distributor kit is more than worth the investment.

Now without trying to be too salesy, I will let you make that decision for yourself. You can visit our website at www.yesweave.com and learn more about our distributor program.

Other benefits of dropshipping

The start-up costs are small: In order to set up a traditional offline hair shop, a good chunk of capital is usually required to buy your inventory of products that you wish to sell from your shop. This is most commonly guess work, there's no saying how much stock you'll sell for that month/year so this eliminates having to risk your money in unsold stock.

You can offer items almost instantly: Usually when a retailer wants to start selling a product, they'll have to wait until all of their wholesale stock has been shipped prior to selling them on their website. Using drop shipping means that when you decide you want a product on your site, you can start advertising and selling almost immediately - after all you do not need to hold any inventory.

You can offer a wider range of products: Having the ability to offer a wider range of products is always something a company can aspire to and with drop shipping, it's possible. You don't have to worry about different colours or sizes and where all that hair is going to be stored, you simply list them on your website and you supplier can deal with the rest.

Testing new products without a risk: When adding new products to your range, the risk of not selling is always an underlying risk. Having to guess what your customers want to buy is a tricky feat for anyone, so being able to test the water without making any huge investment is always an advantage for you.

Time saving is key: Organising your stock and preparing it for delivery can often be a time-consuming nightmare. Using a third party to ship items saves handling, labelling, packing, shipping etc, leaving you time to focus on growing your business in different areas.

HOW DROPSHIPPING WORKS

So now we've talked about dropshipping, you are probably wondering how it all really works. Now assuming you are interested in selling wigs for example but have no money to purchase stock beforehand. Here's an example on how it works;

1. You find a wholesaler who sells the wigs you are interested in reselling.

2. Find out if they offer dropshipping services.

3. Let's assume the wig is currently being sold at a cost price of $40 on the wholesaler's website.

4. You then copy the product details and description from the wholesalers' website and paste it on your own website. Except you set it at a higher retail sale price of say $100.

5. A customer visits your website and purchases the wig from you paying you $100 and the money goes straight into your bank account.

6. You then go back to the wholesalers' site and place an order but this time using the customers' details as the shipping address, and only paying for the wholesale cost price of $40.

7. The wholesaler then ships wig directly to your customer **whilst you gain a profit of $60.**

So your job is essentially to promote these products on your own website setting your own higher price, then pass your customers' details to the supplier after they purchase from you. Imagine you sell about 10 of this single product, then you have just made yourself $600 (60 X 10) for just one product.

And guess what, you did not have to risk any money buying inventory, handling any stock or delivery. All you did was send customers to a wholesaler who handled all the hard work. As you can see, the earning potential with dropshipping is endless. It's just up to you how many products you will love to sell and how much money you want to make.

Of course one of the biggest problems with dropshipping is not having physical access to your products, which can get you questioning the quality of the products your customers are receiving. A great way to get around this is order some samples for yourself first, try them and test the quality yourself. And if they pass the test, you can start reselling these on your website too.

HOW MUCH INVENTORY DO YOU NEED?

There is no set in stone amount of inventory required for a successful hair business. It really depends on which products you plan to sell.

For example, if selling human hair bundles, the decision will be based on a combination of the popular curl patterns which are straight, body wave and curly. From my experience, the bestselling lengths have been between a 14 - 20 inches. However it's always best to try and test out what your customers are ordering the most, then invest more on what works.

Secondly, this will also depend on your budget and how much capital you have to invest in your business. So always go with what you can afford - nothing is too small or too big, just get started.

The problem however is, most wholesale suppliers expect you to buy a minimum of hundreds of units per piece in bulk. However there are still a few wholesalers out there who offer smaller bulk orders. Do not be scared to communicate with and strike a deal with your suppliers for smaller bulk orders. I've personally done this before with some of my vendors who had no issues selling smaller bulk orders.

Again if you are working with dropshipping suppliers, this usually tends to be easier especially given the fact that, they tend to sell individual units rather than in bulk thereby making it easier for you to order samples in the quantities that suit you with no bulk minimum requirements.

INVENTORY MANAGEMENT

Inventory management is defined as the branch of business management concerned with planning and controlling inventories. The role of inventory management is to maintain the desired stock level of specific products or items (Toomey, 2012).

Inventory management is another vital part of running your hair business and something you will need to do on an ongoing basis. Inventory management can help you with keeping accurate track and control of your stock.

Most website dashboards out there already have systems in place that allow you to manage and control stock, however these functionalities are limited and you may require a separate software to keep accurate track of your inventory.

A great software to look into for managing inventory is **Shopventry** which comes with different prices from $39 per month. They also have a free package which comes with a few restrictions. However, if you are looking for a more cost effective inventory management template to maintain your stock, then I recommend the **No Hassle Accounting** inventory template which only comes at a **one off fee of £29.99**.

This is an Excel based inventory management program which we have personally used to keep track of our inventory and has worked a treat over the years.

Part 5

YOUR HAIR BUSINESS WEBSITE

WHY YOU NEED A WEBSITE

So now we have a niche and hopefully some ideas on what vendors to use: be it through buying wholesale or dropshipping, it's time to start thinking about finding a platform to sell your hair – **YOUR WEBSITE.**

Your website is the next most important thing to consider for your new hair brand – so what better place to sell your products than on your own website. A business without a website should be prepared to lose out on over 95% of its customers. Nowadays, people go on the internet 24/7 searching for all types of information. With technology practically taking over the world, it is vital that you have a business website. A business without a website is like building a house without a foundation. Without the internet, there is no way you would have stumbled on this book in the first place. So you can imagine how many customers you could lose if you don't have a website for your business.

Secondly owning a website will save you so much time, money and energy in your day to day activities. Gone are the days where you had to open 100 stores in 100 different cities, just to appeal to customers worldwide. With a website, your laptop and access to the internet, you are on the "World Wide Web" and customers can access and purchase your products from just that one little website.

To get your website up and running you will need 3 key things; **a domain name**, **a hosting platform** and **some design skills** (if you plan to do it on your own) or hire someone to do it for you.

YOUR DOMAIN NAME

Your domain name is the name of your business. It is best to name your domain after your business name. So assuming your online store is called Sandra's Hair, then your domain name could be something in the lines of www.sandrashair.com, or, co.uk, .net, etc. basically what name best suits you.

You can get a domain name registered for less than $10 per year from Namecheap. However if you have another domain provider in mind, you can still use them. If you want to focus on for example UK based customers only, then you could look into a .co.uk domain name. Although a .com name is highly recommended as this is great especially for attracting a global audience.

If your particular domain name isn't available, you should usually get a few suggestions on different names you could use.

Make sure you choose a good and catchy name and remember not to make it too long. If your domain name is too long, people will lose patience trying to type it all out in their browsers, and/or could end up misspelling it.

So come up with something short, sweet and easy to remember. Once you purchase your domain name, this should usually be LIVE instantly and available for at least a year.

BEST WEBSITE HOSTING PLATFORMS

Once your domain name is registered, you need to think about some web hosting options in-order to start creating your website. A domain name without a host is like building a house without a roof. There are several platforms out there which you can use to host your website.

One of the best platforms especially for beginners struggling to create their own hair websites is Shopify. Shopify is not only great for ecommerce online stores, but is also very beginner and user friendly.

Shopify starts at **$29** per month with a 14 Day FREE trial giving you the opportunity to try them out before you make a purchase decision. You can get started with Shopify by CLICKING HERE or visiting www.shopify.com

Other ecommerce platforms you could look into include;

- www.bigcartel.com
- www.bigcommerce.com
- www.webs.com
- www.freewebstore.com
- www.wix.com

However be wary that most free platforms come with so many restrictions and sometimes your website may end up looking rather tacky.

You really do get what you pay for

Again if you join as a Yes Weave Distributor, you instantly gain access to your own ecommerce website with FREE web hosting included.

Examples of what your store is likely to look like if you join our program can be found at;

- www.store.yesweave.com
- demo.store.yesweave.com

SECURING YOUR WEBSITE

Ever stumbled upon a website and was presented with the message stating the website is **"Not Secured"**, then advising you that your personal information in unsafe and could be stolen by attackers? How did you feel about browsing through that website or most of all keying in your email, credit card details to pay for anything on a not secured website?

Let me guess, you probably freaked out and left the website as soon as you could right? Would you want your customers presented with a **Non-Secured** message every time they visit your website?

Well this is exactly what an SSL certificate helps prevent you from. The primary function of any SSL certificate is to secure your website through encrypting the data that passes between your website and the computer of the person viewing your website. The data passed could be usernames, passwords, personal information or even credit card information. This is also a great way to build more trust with your customers who are likely to feel more secure when purchasing from you.

Moreover, Google now ranks websites with an SSL certificate better than unsecured websites meaning your customers can find you even quicker when they search on Google. Most domain name and hosting companies provide you with SSL Certificates, however you have to go through the process of installing that onto your website yourself, which can become a rather technical and complicated process for you. Some hosting platforms like Shopify also issue SSL Certificates as part of their package which can also be beneficial to you. Our Distributor websites at Yes Weave also come with a FREE SSL certificate included. Alternatively you can easily purchase an SSL Certificate at only $49 per year by visiting:

https://www.easyclickwebsites.com/ssl-certificate

This also includes the installation onto your hosting absolutely FREE if you are hosting your website through them. So it is highly recommended that you invest in an SSL Certificate and save yourself the inconvenience of losing sales due to customers leaving your website. Alternatively, if you decide to use a different hosting platform, ensure that they offer SSL certificates as part of their hosting.

PAYMENT PROCESSORS

To sell online, you will need a payment processor that allows customers to pay you instantly. When setting up your ecommerce website, there are a few payment options you could look into to ensure your customers can quickly and easily pay for their transactions online. A few recommended payment processors that are great for your online store are;

PayPal

This is one of the best and safest payment processors to use. It is FREE to register for an account, you can then link your bank account to your PayPal account easily and transfer any payments received from customers directly into your bank account when ready.

You can also pay for transactions online quickly using your PayPal account instead of having to key in your bank details all the time. You can register for a FREE Business Account with PayPal at www.paypal.com. PayPal charges you a small percentage of 3.4% and **20p ($0.30)** on every payment made into your PayPal account. However this isn't substantial considering your transactions are safe and secure.

Stripe

Similar to PayPal is another payment processor known as "Stripe". Stripe is equally great for collecting and processing online transactions directly from your website. All funds paid into your stripe account however are only automatically cleared and deposited directly into your bank account after 7 days. This means unlike

PayPal, you cannot instantly deposit money into your bank account as and when you please, but rather have to wait for their timelines for payments to automatically clear.

Stripe is great in that it allows customers to pay you quickly via your website using their debit or credit card details with no requirement to register for an account prior to payment, as with the case of PayPal. Stripe also charges a transaction fee of 1.4% + 20p for all European cards and **2.9%** for all non-European cards.

Of course there are many more payment processors you could look into such as Square which is great for accepting all major credit cards and allows you to collect offline payments.

IMPORTANT PAGES FOR YOUR ECOMMERCE STORE

When setting up your ecommerce website, there are a few key pages that are essential you have on your website to make information easily accessible to your website visitors and make their browsing experience as smooth and easy as possible. The last thing you want is a website set up with too many irrelevant pages that could confuse your customers and send them to your competitor websites.

Home

Your homepage is the first page customers will see when they first visit your website. So it is essential that the information on your homepage immediately tells customers what your niche is, and what type of products you are selling.

For example with our website www.yesweave.com the homepage immediately tells our website visitors that the brand is geared towards starting a hair business.

So if a website visitor was interested in say electronics then there will be no need wasting time on our website. So be clear on what your brand represents and if possible have a welcome message on your homepage summarising what you do, but try not to have too much jargon on that first page as it could send people away. After all you are running an ecommerce website and not a blog, so less content and more products.

About Us

This is another great page to have so your customers can get a little personal and easily find out more about your brand and what it stands for. Remember when people stumble upon your website, they don't know who you are, where you are based, etc. Hence an about us page builds that trust with customers. It is also a great page to outline your vision, mission and values as a brand.

Product Page

Your website is an ecommerce store which sells products, hence it is important to have a product page or Shop page where people can quickly and easily browse for the products they are interested in.

Shipping & Delivery

Another vital part of an online store is making it clear to your customers how long shipping will take as this will greatly influence their buying decision. Therefore having a page with clear information on shipping times is extremely useful to have on your online store. This will save you a lot of headaches in the future too.

Contact Us

Another vital part of an online store is having a contact page with your contact details where customers can easily reach out to you and communicate in case of any problems or in case they need more information.

Refund Policy

Having a refund policy on your website is another great way to clarify your processes to your customers and avoid any future disappointments.

Whether you offer a 14 day, 28 day or no refund policy, remember to make this clear on your website so customers are aware of it prior to purchasing.

Shopping Cart

Pages such as My Account, Cart and Checkout are also extremely useful to have on your website Menu. This means customers can easily navigate between browsing products, adding them to their carts and checking out without any difficulties.

Other useful pages to have on your website include, **Terms & Conditions and Privacy Policy pages**.

PRICING YOUR PRODUCTS

Pricing refers to how much you charge for your products and/or services. How much you price your products will usually depend on the market, your brand, competition, target audience and other factors.

Assuming you want to sell a Wig at $100, it will be wise to first of all see what competitors are pricing for a similar product in order to determine the right price point. You do not want to end up too cheap or too expensive as you could end up making so many sales but no profits to boast of (if too cheap), or no sales at all (if too expensive).

So try and find the right fit in alignment with your market and industry. As a rule of thumb, you should be able to make at least a minimum of double and a half (2.5) the wholesale price (what you paid for the product).

For example, if you purchased a wig from your supplier for $45 cost price, then you want to charge at-least $112.5 ($45 X 2.5) and above for that product. Remember you have to take into account the cost of other expenses such as packaging, shipping, etc so you don't end up under cutting yourself.

Such a simple pricing strategy will work well for mass produced type products which are bought in bulk and readily available in the market.

Premium pricing is another great approach which works best for certain products. For example, raw hair is more expensive to source and therefore the selling prices tend to be higher.

Or if you are making custom made wigs, again you can charge a premium price for this service since it is more of a VIP service which is unique to you as a brand.

Finally, pricing will depend vastly on your brand, its mission, its vision, the type of products you plan on selling, the audience you want to appeal to, and how you intend to source them.

So make sure you research on market prices, plan your pricing strategy prior to purchasing any wholesale products so you don't end up at a financial loss.

HANDLING SHIPPING

Another vital part of your online hair business is making it clear to your customers how long shipping will take as this is likely to greatly influence their buying decision. If dropshipping, make sure your shipping rates and times mirror those of your suppliers so you do not end up capping down on your profits.

So if your dropshipping supplier is offering a shipping fee of $4.99, make sure this is the same shipping rate on your website or at least incorporated within your price.

If you plan on buying wholesale and reselling, then you can calculate how much it will cost you to package and post each order out to your customers. You can also offer FREE shipping, through incorporating the cost of shipping in your actual products price.

For example, if selling a wig for $100 with a shipping cost of $4.99, you could charge the wig at $105 plus free shipping. In doing so, you still get to keep your profits.

This is a great way to entice customers to buy your products as some people are automatically drawn to free shipping. Try not to make your shipping costs too high or shipping times too slow as this could put your customers off.

Great platforms you could use for your shipping include **https://www.parcel2go.com** to or **Shipstation**.

Part 6

BRANDING & PACKAGING

BUSINESS LOGO

A Logo is extremely vital in building your image and key to branding your business. Your Logo will make you appear a lot more professional, bigger and more established to your audience. This is what differentiates you from competitors and helps you stand out from the crowd.

When you combine a brand with a business name and a logo you have three of the most powerful marketing pieces of a business. When a customer, employee, vendor, lender sees either one of them and they recognize it, you evoke an emotional response, be it good or bad. Deciding on a business logo may not be a quick process. Additionally, you may welcome professional help. My suggestion is to not rush into this piece if you don't have the time or can't find exactly what you want (Rogerson, 2011).

Although having so many different colours to make your logo stand out could sound tempting, it could also end up looking tacky.

Simplicity is key when it comes to designing a logo and it is strongly recommended that you hire a professional to help you decide on the best way to design your logo.

The logo for our brand **Yes Weave** for example has a very clean but unique feel to it. It has a feminine colour - purple which represents the target audience of women with the image at the centre representing hair extensions.

You can get a logo created yourself for free on platforms like Canva.com. However if you are not so good at design, it is highly recommended to get a professional to do it for you on platforms such as www.fiverr.com and www.upwork.com

BUSINESS CARDS & FLYERS

Another powerful way of branding your business and letting people know about your hair company is using business cards and flyers.

Your business cards and flyers will normally contain all your business information including your company name, address, website, email, social media info, phone number and all they need in-order to locate you.

Business cards and flyers can also help to enhance the personal image of a businessperson. Production and printing costs of business cards are low, they are extremely portable and benefits are high, as they make a statement in the business world. As a result, the market value of business cards is high.

The information on your business cards and flyers should reflect the nature of your business so that people do not have to guess what it is that the card is for or what business it represents. You may like the idea of a very stylish logo and simple design, but you want to be sure that anyone who looks at your business card knows why they would be contacting your business.

You should always have especially your business cards handy at all times and make sure that when you strike up a conversation with anyone that you hand them your business card and/or flyers. A great place to get your business cards done cheaply and professionally is at www.vistaprint.co.uk or www.vistaprint.com. So get yourself a business card and distribute them to as many places and people as you possibly can.

PRODUCT PHOTOGRAPHY

Taking pictures of products for your website is another vital part of branding and advertising. You have a few options when it comes to branding photography for your hair business.

HIRE A PHOTOGRAPHER & MODEL

You can either model your hair by yourself or get a model to wear your hair. Easiest way to get some inventory for your photoshoots is to first of all order a few samples from your supplier in a good length (16-20 inches work well) that showcase your textures to customers. You will then need to hire a professional photographer to take these pictures for you.

However do bear in mind that this option is very expensive, especially given the fact that most photographers charge per number of pictures, but can be worth the investment in the long run. Another alternative to using models is to lay the hair on a flat surface or make wigs out of the hair bundles and use mannequins.

TAKE THE PICTURES YOURSELF

You could also save costs by using friends and family to model for you or hire a volunteer model looking to build their modelling portfolio to do it for you at no extra charge. Alternatively, if you are good at photography, then you can also do so yourself or reach out to photography students looking to build their portfolio to work with. For my hair brand Yes Weave for example, I actually got a friend to model the hair for me whilst we took the pictures. I invested in some backdrop, camera, lighting, and then she did her own make up, we got a few hair bundles sewn into wigs and she modelled them all.

Finally I edited the pictures and posted them on the website. These pictures have worked perfectly well in marketing the hair brand over the years and still do.

However our team are now looking into upgrading into more professional shoots sometime by the end of this year. But this could definitely be a great start for your online store.

USE SUPPLIERS PICTURES

Another easier option is to start using your suppliers' stock images. This works well if you plan on drop shipping as you will usually have that automatic permission to use their images anyway. For example, our distributors also have rights to use our images, so if you've seen our images on other hair websites, then it's most likely one of our distributors.

For those buying wholesale, you will need to seek permission from your suppliers to use their pictures.

USING INFLUENCERS IMAGES

When I launched Yes Weave back in 2016, we worked with a few influencers for a couple of months to get the word out there.

What I did was send them out hair products for FREE, they then took pictures, did video reviews on Youtube and then posted on their social media platforms. We were then able to use this information for marketing on our website, social media pages, etc.

This was a great way to create that initial buzz for my brand and really worked a treat in getting those first few clients.

So this is another powerful way to get people wearing your products and using their images on your website to sell your products. This option is also great for marketing but might be an expensive option if you have to use influencers for every single product on your website given the fact that you need to send out so many free products, etc. Nevertheless it is worth a try!

PACKAGING ESSENTIALS FOR YOUR HAIR BUSINESS

Similar to your logo, packaging plays a key role when it comes to branding your business. It acts as a visual representation of your brand and what your customers will see when they purchase your products, and how they will identify and remember you.

Packaging design is the connection of form, structure, materials, colour, imagery, typography and regulatory information with ancillary design elements to make a product suitable for marketing (Klimchuk & Krasovec, 2013).

Packaging is very essential when buying wholesale and reselling products on your own online store, or hand making your own products. With dropshipping, the suppliers deal with the packaging and shipping, however if you are keen on packaging products with your own information, then you can either send your packaging to your suppliers to use on your customer products *(if they offer this service)* or get them to send products out to you first, and then you re-package and ship out to your customers yourself.

This usually works a treat, however be wary that it might be slightly more costly for you especially given the fact that, you will need to pay for additional shipping to finally get the products out to the customers.

Some packaging and shipping must have essentials are highlighted next:

Label Printer

You can get it from Amazon or EBay

3 IN 1 Epson Printer

You can get it from Amazon or EBay

Invoice Template

FREE at: https://www.invoicesimple.com

Flyers, Business Cards & Thank you Cards

https://www.vistaprint.com/

Silk Bonnets, Label Tags, Hair Packaging

http://zazzle.com
https://www.etsy.com

Poly Mailers

You can purchase these on EBay or Amazon

Shipping Scales

You can purchase these on EBay or Amazon

Part 7

MARKETING & ADVERTISING

WEAR YOUR BRAND

This is a great marketing strategy for promoting and advertising your hair business. The truth is, people are ten times more likely to buy from you if you personally use the products you sell. After all why should they trust buying human hair from you if you wear synthetic hair? Why should they buy a lace front wig from you when all you wear is braided hair? This is not to say you should use or wear every single product you sell on your store, but if you can carry at least a piece of your brand with you in some form, this could be extremely beneficial to your business.

Wearing your brand is a pull marketing strategy in that it pulls customers to you rather than you constantly pushing products out to their faces.

Now assuming you have an online store selling lace front wigs, and then decide to wear one of them for an event.

Whilst at the event, someone suddenly walks to you and compliments your hair asking you where you got it done? You can then refer them to your website, hand them your business card to go purchase theirs too.

Now you've just won yourself a customer who was pulled to your product through you merely wearing your brand - and this happened with no extra marketing effort.

Imagine if 3 other people fell in love with your hair, that's even more money in your pocket. So always find a way to wear or try and incorporate your brand everywhere you go with you!

COLLABORATING WITH INFLUENCERS

In this new digital era, collaborating with social media influencers is now becoming a part of every company's digital marketing strategy. Social media influencers are typically people with a huge social media following or fans, be it on Facebook, Instagram, Youtube etc. Think of them as social media celebrities!

Because influencers already have a large following of fans who trust them, companies benefit greatly from working with them through getting quick and fast exposure. The goal however is to work with influencers who are relevant to your niche.

So assuming that you have an online store targeting women with afro hair, then ideally you want to work with afro hair influencers since they are most relevant to your niche.

To get started working with influencers around your niche, you can visit a popular social media platforms such as **Instagram**. Next do a search on: #hairinfluencer or other keywords around your niche. This should bring up different images. Click on the images, then visit the relevant pages to see how popular they are and what engagement their profile is getting through comments, likes and views.

Next check their Instagram bio to see what they do and how you can get in touch with them.

You can also check your competitors' pages and see what type of influencers they currently use. Then see how you too can reach out to those influencers to work with you.

Next, get in touch with a number of them either via Instagram directly or if they have a contact email on their bio, drop them an email introducing your business and find out if they will be happy to promote your business in return for some FREE hair?

Chances are they will always say YES. After all who doesn't want a freebie right? Once they receive the product, all they have to do is take some pictures and post on their page, referring all their fans to your business to purchase the products.

Do bear in mind that some of the larger and more established influencers may charge you a fixed fee to promote your company to their audience - but this could be a powerful way to gain brand exposure quickly. Always remember to do your due diligence on any large influencers before you pay them money to promote your products as a large following doesn't always equal more sales or conversions. See how well other posts advertising brands are performing – are they getting many likes and most importantly do the comments tell you their fans are engaging with what they are advertising?

You can also do a YouTube search on your relevant niche and you should find a few different YouTube channels that produce content around your business area. Use search terms such as your niche then the term **reviews** after your key term, e.g. hair reviews, wig reviews, etc.

This will bring up Youtube channels of influencers currently reviewing other products around your niche. Again see how well their engagements are, are people leaving comments showing any interest on the hair?

USE ETSY

If you don't already know, Etsy is perfect for handmade and custom made products. So if you are into making custom wigs, then there is no better place to market your hair business than on Etsy. Etsy currently has over 30 million buyers constantly searching for products like the one you currently sell thereby indicating a great potential for you as a business owner.

The good news is, it's free to join Etsy and you can get started by simply visiting their website at www.etsy.com

Next register for a FREE account, take some good product images, key in detailed item descriptions and as start listing those products for sale.

POP UP SHOPS

Pop Up shops are another powerful way to promote and market your new hair business. Pop-up retail is the temporary use of physical space to create a long term, lasting impression with potential customers.

A pop-up shop allows you to communicate your brand's promise to your customers through the use of a unique and engaging physical environment while creating an immersive shopping experience (Shopify, 2018).

Truth is there are a lot of people that still want to see, feel, and touch products prior to purchasing them. And having a pop up shop offers just that.

To set up a pop up shop you need to start by researching on pop ups happening in your local area, then get in touch with the venues to secure a space.

Alternatively if there are no pop ups in your area, why not set up your own pop up? Simply rent some space and invite other businesses to promote themselves - at a small fee of course. Then promote your event as much as you can and get the ball rolling.

Get your hair bundles (or samples) together with your flyers, business carts, mannequins or display unit and promote that business to your customers. This also works great with dropshipping as you can get people to feel the samples, then pre-order lengths of their choice and have them delivered

INSTAGRAM

Instagram is an online service in video-sharing, photo-sharing and social networking that enables you to take pictures and videos and applying filters to them. You can edit the photos and essentially communicate with your customers via images and video making it a very powerful marketing platform for your business.

1. To get started with Instagram, simply register for a free account at www.instagram.com and remember to use your business name as your display name.

2. Once registered you will need to start posting some amazing pictures to attract some likes, views and followers to your page. This can be a picture of the products or services you sell, your blog content etc.

3. Next use hashtags (#) under each post to attract as much engagement as possible. Say for example your business is on wigs, then you could post your picture then use popular hashtags around that niche such as; #lacefrontwigs #humanhair #fbrazilianhairwig, etc. under that picture to attract new likes, views and followers.

To find out what hashtags are trending in your niche, simply do a search on Instagram with your hashtag and relevant keyword e.g (#lacefrontiwgs) and Instagram will begin to recommend the most popular and highly searched hashtags around your niche.

Now take a note of those popular hashtags and list them under your own pictures. This means anyone going on Instagram looking for anything hair related will most likely stumble on your account and eventually follow you. The more followers you get, the more your brand is known and the more exposure it gets.

A second way to gain engagement fast is to look at your competitors accounts, then find out who their followers are, next follow their followers and in return they will begin to follow you too. This might take a while initially, but can get you so many free and unique visitors to your page and consequently to your business.

Another way to gain engagement fast on Instagram is to follow accounts of other people who are interested in for example hair, and engage with them on their pages. The more you engage with others, the more they engage back with you and get to know about you. Think of it as cross-promotion.

A few final tips;

- Don't like so many pictures within an hour (e.g. liking over 100 pictures per hour could get Instagram to think you are spamming and in the unfortunate circumstances might block your account).

- Don't post pictures promoting products or services all the time. Mix and match both formal and informal pictures. Memes, quotes, in addition to pictures promoting your blog or affiliate products are the best way to go.

- Be consistent! Post at-least once a day , like pictures of people with an interest in your niche. Even comment in their pictures to draw even more attention back to your own page.

If you need more help advertising with Instagram then checkout the **Marketing for Boutiques and Online Stores** at the Income Reap Academy. Again this training is included FREE with the Yes Weave Distributor Membership.

PINTEREST

Pinterest is another powerful way of reaching out to thousands of customers online easily. People go on Pinterest every single day looking for inspiration and ideas on different things, from fashion ideas to weight loss recipes. Content is usually shared in the form of **pins** and **boards.** You can think of your board as an "Album" and your pins as the "Images" within that album.

So how is this beneficial to your business?

Now assuming your hair business was centred on "virgin hair bundles", then what you could do is register for a free Pinterest account and upload product images from your website.

This means if someone went on Pinterest (or even google) searching for hair bundles, then your pins or boards are likely to show up, thereby linking them back to your website and consequently winning you a new customer.

This works just like search engine optimization and can generate ongoing FREE website traffic for your business every single day.

To get started with Pinterest, register for a FREE account at: https://www.pinterest.com. Once registered, you can begin creating boards and pins with your images and relevant content. You can upload product images directly from your website into your Pinterest boards.

Remember to use the right titles and descriptions on your products in order to attract your target audience who are likely to find you easily not only through Pinterest, but also from doing Google searches.

Each time you have some new products on your online store, remember to upload some product pins in your account to link them back to your online store.

If you need more help advertising with Pinterest then checkout the **Marketing for Boutiques and Online Stores** at the Income Reap Academy. Again this training is included FREE with the Yes Weave Distributor Membership.

FACEBOOK

Facebook is a social network and micro-blogging platform with a leading social community online. As a matter of fact, there are currently over 1.6 billion active users on Facebook. Having a Facebook page for your business is a great way to build relationships with existing clients, communicate with them, win new clients, interact and engage with all your customers. Once people are able to relate with you, winning those customers to your business and making sales will be easier than you think.

Facebook is free to join and also very search engine friendly. The truth is google will sometimes target your Facebook page even better than your website. This means opening your Facebook page with your business name will ensure your business is ranked at the top of

Google.

"Why not try this and see how fast google ranks your business". Compared to other traditional advertising strategies out there, Facebook is not only free to use but is a cheaper way to advertise your business to an even wider audience. Not only do you attract a wider audience, you can easily track performance to see how well your ads are performing and where traffic is coming from.

One of the greatest things about advertising with Facebook, is the flexibility of your advertisements. You can customize your advertisements so they appear only to specific groups or segments of people based on the information contained within their profile or based on gender, location or personal preference.

Getting Started on Facebook

In-order to start advertising your business on Facebook, you must first of all create a personal Facebook account. Once you have a personal account set up then open a business page on Facebook.

1. If you don't already have a Facebook account, register a FREE account at www.facebook.com. You will then be prompted to complete all the relevant information to enable you to create an account. Please **DO NOT** use your personal account for business.

2. Once you create a personal account, the next step is to create a business page. Click on the drop down Arrow at the top Right hand of the page and click on **"Create Page"**.

3. You can then select the relevant page from

business, brand, company etc., depending on your business type.

4. Fill out all the relevant information about your business, brand or company. On the **"enter an address for your page field"** type in your exact company name. This will ensure your business page is properly ranked by Google.

5. Next upload a profile picture for your business. If you are a company or brand, then your logo is usually the best option. If your face is your brand, then a good professional picture of you should do the trick.

6. Next add a great cover picture on your page. Make sure your cover picture is professionally designed and can stand out in order to attract customers and people to your page.

Guess What? You have just created your Facebook page for your business in just minutes.

You can advertise through Facebook using three different ways;

Freely – promote your Facebook page to your existing customers and grow your page organically.

Facebook Ads – pay Facebook to attract millions of customers for you on your behalf.

Facebook Groups – Join groups similar to your niche, participate with others and use that to promote your services.

Once you have your page created, the next step is to invite your customers, clients and friends to like your page. You can easily get fans and followers to your Facebook page by connecting your Facebook page to your website.

This means your website visitors get to find your

new Facebook page and like it. If you already have friends on Facebook, you could also invite your friends to like your page and get them to spread the word. Now it's time to start posting on Facebook and attracting some new fans to your page. Be aware that opening a Facebook page for the sake of just opening a page won't drive any customers to your business. In fact you are better off not opening a page in the first place if you intend to just abandon it and expect sales.

If you need more help advertising with Facebook then checkout the **Marketing for Boutiques and Online Stores** at the Income Reap Academy. Again this training is included FREE with the Yes Weave Distributor Membership.

EMAIL MARKETING

Email marketing is a **solid form** of marketing and one that will bring you recurring customers over and over and over again. You obtain their emails and send deals, offers, discounts, promotions to keep them up to date with everything going on.

But how do you get these customers in the first place? One easy way of getting them is asking them to subscribe on your website for updates. This process of getting customers to your list is called **list building.**

List building is vital for every online business. It is the most effective way of building loyalty and trust with your visitors in the long term. Truth is, most people will come to your website and when they leave, you will never hear back from them ever again or even know they ever visited your website in the first place.

However, with list building you can capture their email addresses and get to keep these customers for GOOD. The list building process is used by a lot of multi-million dollar companies to get customers and definitely a marketing strategy I highly recommend.

A great way to capture people's attention fast is to offer something for FREE or a discount on your services. Truth is people love freebies and once they see the word FREE, they won't hesitate to grab or come running for those products or services.

If you are selling products, you can give them offers like - first time discounts to bring them to your business. If you have something that requires monthly payments, why not give them 1 free month subscription to entice them, before you know it they will enjoy the free service so much they will be happy to pay to continue enjoying those benefits.

For your hair store, you could offer your

customers a discount code in exchange for their email addresses. That way they can sign up to receive a discount off their first order. That's exactly the same way list building works.

For this to work, you will first of all need an autoresponder. An autoresponder will help you automatically deliver your incentive via email marketing to your subscribers once they subscribe. A great autoresponder software I will highly recommend is Aweber.

Aweber allows you to create pop ups and opt in forms, and automates the email marketing process for you. Once you have an autoresponder, it's time to create your pop up or sign up form on your website.

This is simply a little box asking users for their name and email address in exchange for your free incentive above. Once they confirm their subscription, they will then become stored in your list and you can send them regular emails, new product releases, courses, updates and other useful information.

This is also used to build strong relationships with your subscribers. Remember you are NOT selling them anything yet but giving them something for free in exchange of their name and email address. And within this FREE product, you are then convincing them to buy your main product.

If you need more help using Email Marketing, then checkout the **Marketing for Boutiques and Online Stores** at the Income Reap Academy. Again this training is included FREE with the Yes Weave Distributor Membership.

GOOGLE

Google as you would already know is the largest search engine in the world. Truth is, you probably stumbled on this book from doing a google search on how to start a hair company. So imagine the millions and billions of people worldwide, who are searching for information every single day on google. "How to lose weight", "how to stop smoking", "how to make money", "how to cure eczema" etc. Google has all types of information anyone could imagine. There are several ways to advertise using Google, such as: using *Google AdWords and Google Search Console.*

Google AdWords is a quick and fast way to attract customers to your new business. Google AdWords helps you advertise your website, by spreading it on the internet to customers interested in your market. Instead of you doing all the hard work trying to find out where to advertise your business, google does it all for you and gets all the customers for you whilst you sit back and relax. Businesses pay google to advertise for them through Google AdWords, meaning whenever people click on your website through google, you pay google per click. Again if you have some capital to invest, then I will recommend you try this method by registering for an account at www.adwords.google.com

Google Search Console is another great FREE way of making your website or blog visible on google. Think of it like the yellow pages where businesses are included in a catalogue and distributed to all addresses in that city or location.

This will ensure that your website is easily visible when people do a google search, your website or blog is likely to appear. You can get started by visiting:

https://www.google.com/webmasters/tools/submit-url.

Once google reviews and approves this, they will then include your website in their directory.

REFERRALS

Referrals are a method of spreading the word by telling a friend to tell a friend. Let people know about your new hair business and let your friends tell others about your business. Referral marketing is a structured and systematic process to maximize word of mouth potential.

Referral marketing does this by encouraging, informing, promoting and rewarding customers and contacts to think and talk as much as possible about their supplier, their company, product and service and the value and benefit the supplier brings to them and people they know. Word of mouth is potentially the best form of marketing for a business and best of all, is probably the most cost effective! Also known as viral marketing, word of mouth lets your customers do the promotion for you which is the best recommendation that anyone can get. The best way to get people talking about your services is to give them value first.

The best sources for your referrals are your existing customers – these are the people who are loyal to you and have trusted you well enough to purchase from you. A few ways to get them to refer your brand is to offer them customers' discounts and rewards each time they refer a new friend to your hair company. Alternatively get them to leave reviews in exchange for an incentive.

That is how you get word of mouth going and get the attention of potential clients. Thereafter, it's just a matter of building a friendly relationship (not hard selling) with the people you meet and/or already know. You'll be amazed at how easy it is and what great connections you'll make, along with the opportunities that will open up and bring you more clients!

FINALLY...

Remember these marketing strategies are all powerful in their own right. You do not necessarily need to implement all these strategies but rather focus on the strategies that are working best for your business. If you require more in-depth information on how these different marketing strategies work, please visit the <u>Marketing for Boutiques and Online Stores</u> at the Income Reap Academy. Again this training is included FREE with the Yes Weave Distributor Membership.

Part 8

POSITIONING YOURSELF FOR SUCCESS

Did you think we were done?

Well Congratulations on making it this far! Hopefully you should have your new hair business up and running by now - or at least have some ideas to get the ball rolling. You will be pleased to know that, you've officially gone through the most important steps towards officially starting your own hair company and creating that hair empire for yourself and generations to come. Like most business books out there, I could easily end this book right here and leave the rest to you which is fine. However from experience, I can assure you that there is more to business than just coming up with an idea, starting that business and attracting customers.

This is something so many business owners are unaware of, and the reason most people find themselves stuck after starting a business, whilst others give up before they've even started the business.

Now that you finally have a business up and running and some marketing strategies in place, this is sufficient to keep you going. However in-order to run a business successfully, you need to look into effective ways of positioning yourself for long term business success which is exactly what this chapter aims to explore.

STAYING CREATIVE & INNOVATIVE

Coming up with a business idea is a great first step towards tapping into your creative juices. However creativity shouldn't just end at coming up with an idea but you should consistently seek for more innovative ways to improve and grow your business. When innovation and creativity stops in a business, it reflects negatively on business success.

You do not require a special skill or talent in-order to be creative. You can be creative even if you don't think you are - everyone can be creative but you have to be willing to start somewhere and the creative process will become more natural over time. Below are a few tips and habits to help you stay creative in your business.

Make New Connections: Being innovative doesn't require a university degree; it simply requires making a connection between existing ideas. For example a self-service checkout installed in a supermarket doesn't change the idea of the supermarket but rather a process in that existing supermarket.

So look at your existing business or others around you and see how processes could be improved and things done differently.

Think Outside The Box: Many of the products we take for granted today are the result of people thinking outside their limits. e.g. the smartphone is now part of our day to day lives, however it took an innovative and creative person to come up with that idea of changing the way we use our phones.

Ask Questions: Creative thinking goes beyond just solving specific problems or inventing new things. A truly creative mind is always coming up with the questions too, not just the solutions. What questions are you asking to prompt your ideas? The bigger the question, the greater the impact those ideas may have on the world. You can start by addressing smaller problems but don't limit yourself to those.

Think Like A Child: As adults we tend to think in a conditioned way aimed at showing how clever we are. Yet, as children, we were simply spontaneous and far more creative in our thinking. To recapture your childhood curiosity, allow yourself to just wonder at things, to be completely present in the here and now, and to detach yourself from what you thought was real.

Note down your Ideas: Personally my creative juices tend to flow in during the late hours of the night just before I snooze to sleep. What I do is, immediately type out those ideas on my phone notepad because trust me, it is very easy to forget those ideas.

Choose what works best for you and make sure you have a way to record your ideas at all times. You never know when an important idea will surface. Capture all of your ideas - even those that seem impossible to implement at that time, because what seems impossible now may not be impossible in the future.

SETTING GOALS

Goal setting is extremely useful in positioning yourself for business success. Every business has a mission and a vision which you need to be working towards at all times. The moment you lose focus of these goals is the moment your business starts to suffer. Think of a football game for example;

"People play football with the goal of scoring. If there wasn't a goal to score, then football might just be a pointless sport".

So like football setting goals be it for your life, your career or your business is key to achieving long term success. Goals are a great tool for direction and also provide the motivation to get us through difficult times and choices. For example, going to college while working full-time may be stressful and difficult in the short-term, but in the long run being able to pursue the professional goals we desire will make it worthwhile. Goals also serve as the destination for what we really want out of life.

For some people, goals are measured in money or material goods, while for others goals are measured in time or freedom. You will never achieve your goals unless you: *know exactly what you want, are passionate about your goal, and have a solid, realistic plan of action.*

However do not fall into the temptation of only focusing on your long term goals and losing sight of your short term goals. The reason some people find it too hard to achieve their goals is because they tend to set their long term goals, prior to setting their short term goals or simply not planning out their goals carefully. Short-term goals seem to be our starting point for our long term ones and can also motivate one to plan for longer goals, so make sure you start with your short term goals first.

Another important step in goal setting is to identify exactly what your goal is. What will achieving that goal really look like? Be as specific as possible about exactly what your desired end result is. If your goal is to create a more successful business, what will that look like?

Are you thinking in terms of simply hiring someone else to give you more free time? Are you looking for more sales and profit? Regardless of what you want, the best way to get it is to first clarify exactly what you want in as much detail as possible. This may seem like hard work - but without a clear mental picture, you'll never have the focus required to achieve your goal.

Next remember to write down your goals in as much detail as possible. Then ensure that you review and revisit them on a daily to weekly basis because this will encourage and motivate you to achieve them, plus this will also keep that vision of your goal alive.

Sharing your goals with someone you trust or even a mentor is another great way to set goals. By sharing your goals with other people you can get a second opinion which could help you in that journey of success. The problem that usually occurs though is that, some people are just too shy to tell others about their goals for several reasons which is quite understandable.

However, if there's someone you feel you can trust to share your goals with, then do not hold back on another view point.

Finally, remember not to lose track. It is very possible that at some point in your business journey, you might realise that you are not achieving your goals as well or as quickly as you had initially anticipated.

However do not let this discourage you but rather pick up where you left off or find other effective ways to achieve that goal.

TIME MANAGEMENT IS KEY

If you are like me, then you've probably had those moments where it felt like there just wasn't enough hours in the day. So much to do but yet so little time to achieve it all. Somehow there never seems to be enough time to get everything done, especially given the fact that we just have about 16 hours a day not counting 8 hours of sleep. It is therefore important how we use the time we have - especially as entrepreneurs.

From dealing with customer service to managing finances, marketing and advertising - running a business comes with so many hurdles that can make the whole process all too overwhelming for most entrepreneurs.

One has to be committed to fulfil all the responsibilities with 100% perfection and in doing so, people find themselves perplexed as to how to approach and manage all the things and still enjoy ample leisure hours.

Sometimes it may even feel like you are working for hours without any results - especially during the initial stages of your business. As such time management is key and you need to find a way to discipline yourself.

Setting specific working hours is one essential way to overcome this problem. This would provide an outline, on the basis of which further planning would be undertaken especially given that it is so easy to waste time on non-productive tasks unconsciously.

Personally I have a weekly timetable set up with hours of work and what I need to do each day. For example, Monday mornings are for creating content, whilst afternoons are for business improvement processes. However I still occasionally get distracted by client calls and other things which are unavoidable. However, I always find ways to get back on track. Hence, flexibility has to be exercised when managing time, as the actual time taken could be different from planned.

Secondly, set yourself some break hours. It is very easy, especially for us entrepreneurs to spend the whole day and night on our computer screens. There's a reason why even 9-5 jobs come with breaks - because these are great to get yourself out of your desk and recharge your batteries.

Similarly, you should set yourself some hours in the day where you can unwind, relax, go for a walk and just give yourself a break.

Another important aspect of time management is setting priorities to ensure tasks are performed in order of priority.

Prior to me outsourcing my customer service to virtual assistants, I use to spend almost half my day responding to customer queries back and forth. I would feel like I had to respond to those emails as soon as possible otherwise I would lose a potential client.

Now there's a reason why even larger companies have service level agreement (SLA) times. So I decided to set a response time of 48 hours, then created an autoresponder which immediately told my customers their queries will be picked up within that time.

This meant that I could give myself a break, then pick up the queries at the times I had set for myself - trust me those customers can wait especially if their queries are non-urgent! So set specific times during your work hours to open email.

This should usually be the first thing and the last thing you do each work day. If you open your email periodically and respond to it, your work hours can be eaten up in a hurry!

STAYING MOTIVATED

As a business owner, staying motivated can sometimes be one of the hardest things to emulate - especially during those times when it seems business just isn't going as planned. After all how do you really stay motivated when you are so close to losing the will to carry on with that business?

Lack of motivation happens to us all, but if you do not encourage yourself to accept opportunities and be challenged, no one else will. It is most important to keep your eye on the goal, find ways to keep going, and in no time, you shall reap its benefits. The truth is, the biggest things usually happen when we are at the verge of giving up or quitting. After all pain is one of those things that forces people to change.

For example; getting a negative customer review might just be the push you need to improve your business. Not making any sales might actually motivate you to invest more on your marketing and advertising strategies, etc. It may seem like a bitter experience at first but is just the right amount of motivation we need in order to improve our business and even ourselves.

So you need to constantly remind yourself about why you are doing it? Who are you doing it for?

Why are you even running that business or project? What pushed you to start that business in the first place? Is it to create your own business empire, becoming your own boss, quit that stressful job or just spend more time with your family and loved ones? What were those missions and visions you initially set out to achieve?

Do they still stand or have these changed and why? Find something to keep you motivated and always stay focused on that goal. To motivate yourself, sometimes you need to be willing to step out of your comfort zone because success like they say only begins outside your comfort zone. Be willing to push yourself beyond the norm - no matter how strange or abnormal it may seem.

Don't lose focus on your goal and use that to stay motivated. Keep believing in yourself and your ability to achieve success, avoid negativity, toxic people and anything that will hinder your success or hold you back, avoid distractions, hang on to your dreams - they may dangle in there for a moment but these little stars will be your driving force.

Give yourself a break, have enough rest, take sufficient sleep and recharge yourself. Keep trying no matter how hard life may seem and remember winners never quit.

SELF IMPROVEMENT

One of my favourite quotes by Warren Buffett is the one which goes;

"The more you learn the more you earn".

Business is something that is constantly changing especially given the digital era we now live in with constant changes, technological upgrades, new systems, new social media platforms, etc. which can all impact business operations.

The truth is, marketing strategies that worked 4-5 years ago may not be as effective today as they were back in the day. For example, traditional marketing strategies such as cold calling, direct mail marketing are close to non-effective these days due to emerging digital trends such as social media marketing, which has now transformed the way businesses are run and operated.

Online shopping is another trend transforming the way traditional businesses operate. It is very rare to find a business these days that lacks an online presence - and if it does, there's a high chance this could be hindering their sales and growth drastically.

Personally I am constantly investing time and money in learning new skills and working on business improvement through self-development. When I went back to university to complete my Masters in Business Management with Entrepreneurship in 2017, people kept asking me;

"What's the point of doing a masters when you already have thriving businesses up and running?"

My answer always remained, I need to learn more new and transferable skills that could help improve my businesses.

Bear in mind my background was Accounting and Finance, and although I had some experience starting several businesses, I was still lacking on other business areas, hence decided to take on the course. Not only has this course helped exposed me to so many new business strategies, it has also helped with self-development and business improvement.

The truth is starting a business is just the tip of the iceberg, however to run a successful business you need to find ways to constantly learn and improve your skills.

Now I'm not saying you should go back to university and complete a full time master's programme - there is so much freely accessible information around in the form of google, books, online courses, Youtube and so much more.

Just get on Google right now and search for any business related question, and you will be surprised at the amount of FREE information readily available at your fingertips.

My point is if your business is still living in the Stone Age or using outdated practices, you will find yourself left behind and your customers will eventually go to your competitors who are more in tune with external changes. For example with my online courses, I cannot count how many times I've changed and updated its content due to frequent changes around the industry.

So invest a few hours a week learning a new skill that could be beneficial in improving your business. Listen to inspirational speakers, coaches, mentors and other people you look up to in the industry.

What are they doing well and how could you achieve the same for your business? If it means investing in books, courses, training programs to learn and improve your skills, then go for it. Do not underestimate the power of learning for self-improvement and development.

Change is the only constant in life, but one's ability to adapt to it is what will determine your success in life - **Benjamin Franklin**

PRODUCTIVITY IS VITAL

You might have heard of the saying; *"Focus on being productive rather than busy"*. You could be the most hardworking person out there but at the end of the day, productivity depends on how many completed tasks are of good quality. If you do your job right, your overall productivity levels tend to increase. One great way of staying productive is to be organized. This could be achieved through filing and organizing your paperwork, decluttering, keeping a calendar, etc. In doing so you would realise that you are a lot more productive.

If your environment or workplace is cluttered, then this could equally clutter your mind, your thoughts and your decisions. Hence staying organised is an essential part of staying productive.

Procrastination is a killer as they say and can equally hinder your productivity. If you keep postponing tasks and not taking any action, there is no way you can achieve productivity.

Postponing tasks for a day is likely to turn to a week, a month, and eventually never completed. Remember the one thing you can never get back in life is your time. So why waste time procrastinating when you can just get started now! **Too busy?** Well who isn't? There are a lot of people out there busier than you who are still able to achieve things and get things done. The time you spend complaining about being too busy is the same time you could spend doing something productive in your life or business.

How many hours a week do you spend browsing on social media, watching Netflix, TV, going out there socializing with friends or just complaining about being busy? Surely there are a bunch of unproductive things in your life right now that you could substitute with more productive tasks. Now think about that!

Negative influences in your life are another killer of productivity. To attain continuous productivity, it is very important for you to veer away from people who have negative vibes, constantly bring you down, do not support you, or just don't understand your journey.

It is essential to find a good company of people who are all enthusiastic, encouraging, and have a positive outlook in life to help you stay productive. I've realised that, the older I get, the smaller my circle of friends is becoming. This is because I am now in a different phase and journey in my life and this change is equally reflected within my social circle.

A lot of people I knew in school, college are no longer in contact with me and vice versa, simply because we are all at different stages in our lives and pursuing different interests - which is all part of change and growing up.

So if you find yourself still doing the same thing you were doing 5-10 years ago then maybe it's time to revisit your goals and ambitions *(or set some if you don't have one)* see what's going right, wrong or what is simply not working? And ask yourself if you are truly achieving productivity or not? And then start finding ways to achieve it.

And finally, don't forget to look after your health! One thing I will tell you from experience is that an unhealthy mind and lifestyle equals an unproductive one. I remember there were days where I would overwork myself and get little to no sleep whatsoever and this eventually reflected on my health and most of all productivity. Don't try to fight sleep when it comes knocking - it's your body's way of telling you it's had enough and can't process any more. I use to try and fight sleep by drinking lots of caffeine in the hopes that I would stay awake and achieve more.

But the truth is, it was in fact taking me 3-4 hours to complete tasks I'm used to completing in the space of less than an hour - when well rested. So stop lying to yourself that you can be productive despite feeling tired because your brain will never process things as normal or as quickly as it would if you had a good night's rest. It's not worth it! And remember success won't matter if you don't have the good health to enjoy it.

BE PATIENT

One thing so many of us human beings lack is patience and wanting things to happen when, where and how we expect them to happen. When it comes to business, patience is one of the biggest problems and challenges a lot of entrepreneurs are equally faced with.

They start a business today then expect to make their first million by the end of the first month. And when they don't achieve the results they initially anticipated, they quickly give up in search for the next magical quick fix. Success isn't an overnight process and even the few people who eventually make it to the top, had to go through a process to get to that point and level of success.

For example I've been online since 2012 part time back and forth, and it wasn't until around 2016 that my businesses started generating me a full time income which then allowed me to quit my job and focus on my businesses full time. The reason why it took long for me was because I was basically testing the waters and only doing this part time.

Secondly, I had no one to really guide me in the process and pretty much had to learn from my failures and mistakes as I went along. However this process may be different for you and may not take that long for you to start achieving results especially with a book like this one to guide you, and so many resources now available to speed up this process that weren't available when I initially started.

Furthermore, always remember that your money would not automatically start working for you overnight - it may take a day, a week, a month and even a year depending on how well you treat your business and how you chose to implement the relevant strategies.

If things aren't going as planned, don't give up! Just because it isn't working now doesn't mean it's not going to work tomorrow.

Don't quit your day job just yet but rather run your online business part time - evenings and weekends, dedicate a few hours a week building your online business, and as time goes on things will start to fall in place. By keeping your day job, the financial strain isn't too heavy on you either since you can still afford to pay your bills, whilst building additional wealth at the side.

FINAL WORDS OF WISDOM

Although this book is aimed at ensuring that you take action and implement the relevant strategies necessary to start your online hair company, I understand that life can get in the way of most people. So if you get to a point where you find yourself distracted do not worry, simply pick up from where you left off the day before and continue from there. Secondly, I also understand that everyone is different and some people are at different stages in their start up journey and therefore do not expect you to follow each step as described. So feel free to read and use this book as you please – be it in a day, week, month or year. It's really up to you how you choose to read, use and apply it.

Just remember that the end goal here is to TAKE ACTION.

Starting a business may seem overwhelming at first, but I can assure you that it will all be worth it in the end. The most important thing is taking those first steps towards getting started. Thinking or dreaming about starting a business won't make a difference unless you physically take action. We all have the potential to make our dreams come true and live a more financially fulfilling life.

Remember to stay focused, motivated, productive, patient, creative and keep going. Go start that hair business right now, don't get left behind whilst others are achieving success. You can either take no action, and stay where you are right now OR turn your life around and start creating that successful business empire. **The ball is now in your court!**

ACKNOWLEDGEMENTS

Firstly I would like to thank the almighty God for giving me strength and wisdom throughout the process of writing this book. To my amazing parents, family and husband for supporting me morally and emotionally.

To all my clients, students and everyone who has motivated me to write this book – a massive thanks. Finally for all future hair bosses out there reading this book, I hope you find this book useful in helping you start your own online hair company from scratch.

Wishing you all the best in your business journey!

Denise.

ABOUT THE AUTHOR

Denise Fonweban-Ulasi is an online entrepreneur and business coach. She started her first ever online business in 2012 selling information products online, but has since personally founded several online businesses including her online stores **Yes Weave** – an online hair extension company, and her online clothing brand for the business and professional woman - **Fash Vie**. She is also the founder of the **Run Boutique Academy** - an online platform that offers training courses for people looking into starting their own online clothing boutiques from scratch.

She has over 10 years' of combined experience working within in the digital, financial, retail and banking sectors – with 6 years working within the online and digital sectors.

Additionally she holds a first class honours degree in Accounting with Entrepreneurship as well as an Msc Business Management with Entrepreneurship, a Diploma in Digital Marketing, AAT Qualified, and a wide range of experience working with entrepreneurs and start-ups as a digital consultant.

With around 500,000 views on her Youtube channel - the Startup Reine, and so much success in the digital space, her aim is to build a community, inspire and empower others (especially women like her) into starting their own online businesses, creating success in their life and making their money work for them.

IMPORTANT NEXT STEPS

Now that you've read this book, you should have pretty much everything you need to start and launch your own successful hair company. However if you are looking for more help and support with practically getting things set up, then feel free to check us out **Yes Weave**.

Yes Weave is an online platform that helps people start their own hair company through offering a distributor kit, creating your website and offering marketing training resources to help you launch your hair business. With our Distributor business Starter Kit, you have everything you will need to start that hair company.

WIN FREE ACCESS TO THE YES WEAVE BUSINESS KIT

As a thank you and bonus to you for purchasing and reading this book, we are pleased to also offer you **FREE 3 Months Access to our Starter Distributor Membership** (worth $199). You can find out more on what's included by visiting us at www.yesweave.com

For an opportunity to WIN access to this FREE membership, simply follow the 2 steps below;

1. Leave a Review of this Book on Amazon

2. Screenshot your review and email to us at;

support@yesweave.com

Instructions will then be sent to you to claim your

FREE (3 Month Membership Access).

USEFUL RESOURCES

❖ Start Your Hair Business at:

www.yesweave.com

❖ Get business Cards and flyers at:

www.vistaprint.co.uk or

www.vistaprint.com.

- ❖ Register a Domain Name at: Namecheap

- ❖ Get Web Hosting at:

  www.easyclickwebsites.com.

- ❖ Wholesale & Dropshipping Suppliers:

  Alibaba.com, DHGATE.com

- ❖ Create an online store quickly at: Shopify

- ❖ Register Your Business at:

  https://www.irs.gov (USA) or

  https://www.gov.uk (UK)

- ❖ To manage your day to day bookkeeping, you
  can get this affordable bookkeeping software
  at www.nohassleaccounting.com

REFERENCES

LaMonica, P. (2018, February 6). *Amazon worth more than Microsoft for first time*. Retrieved from CNN Money: http://money.cnn.com/2018/02/06/investin g/amazon-microsoft-market-value/index.html

Nelson, E., & Karaian, J. (2018, April 10). *How much is Mark Zuckerberg worth?* Retrieved from QZ.COM: https://qz.com/1248927/what-is-mark-zucke rbergs-net-worth-in-2018/

Mintel. (2017, September 15). *BRITS HUNG UP ON ONLINE FASHION: ONLINE SALES OF CLOTHING, FASHION ACCESSORIES AND FOOTWEAR GROW BY 17% IN 2017*. Retrieved from Mintel Press: http://www.mintel.com/press-centre/fashion

/uk-online-sales-of-clothing-fashion-accessori
es-and-footwear-grow-by-17-in-2017

PRNewswire. (2017, July 5). *The UK Clothing Market
2017-2022*. Retrieved from PRNewswire:
https://www.prnewswire.com/news-releases
/the-uk-clothing-market-2017-2022-3004838
62.html

Winch, J. (2013, April 16). *8m Britons run online
businesses from home*. Retrieved from The
Telegraph:
https://www.telegraph.co.uk/finance/person
alfinance/9997044/8m-Britons-run-online-bu
sinesses-from-home.html

Williams-Grut, O. (2017, October 17). *ASOS sales pass
£1.8 billion as profit jumps 145%*. Retrieved
from Business Insider UK:
http://uk.businessinsider.com/asos-2017-res
ults-sales-profit-revenue-2017-10

www.ingramcontent.com/pod-product-compliance
Lightning Source LLC
Chambersburg PA
CBHW030618220526
45463CB00004B/1334